Swahili Kitchen

Published in 2005 by:
Gallery Publications
P.O. Box 3181, Zanzibar
email: gallery@swahilicoast.com

© 2005 Gallery Publications
Photographs © Javed Jafferji
Text by Elie Losleben

Graphic Designer: Terence Fernandes
Designed by Zanzibar Gallery Publishers

ISBN 9987 667 45 7

Photographs are available for commercial use from Impact
Photos in the UK
e mail: library@impactphotos.com

Dedicated to my aunts Batul and Kulsum Jafferji

Other books in this series:
Zanzibar Style
Voted one of the 'Top 20 travel books for Christmas 2001'
by the UK's Times newspaper.
Zanzibar Style Recipes
Recipes from Zanzibar's top hotels and restaurants.
Safari Living
Showcases Tanzania's top safari lodges and camps.
Safari Living Recipes
Accompanying 'designer' cookbook featuring handpicked
recipes from Tanzania's top safari lodges and camps.
Swahili Style
Covers the design and architecture of the Swahili Coast,
featuring exclusive properties and private homes that
have taken their inspiration from the old stone towns and
coral palaces of the Indian Ocean coastline.

Front cover: The Palms beach.
Back cover, clockwise from the top: Tusitiri Dhow,
Kipungani Explorer, Muniras Camp and Peponi Hotel.

Swahili Kitchen

Text by Elie Losleben
Photographs by Javed Jafferji

Published by Gallery Publications

Contents

Introduction

Walk through the alleyways of an old Swahili stone town in the late afternoon and the smell of spices and fish, coconut milk and rice waft out to meet you from open doorways. Whether you're in Lamu, Zanzibar or Mombasa, skewers of meat or fish *mishkaki*, *madafu* coconut milk drunk straight from the shell or freshly fried *samosa* make tantalising roadside snacks. In the coastal villages, under swaying coconut trees and the shade of looming tamarinds, women clad in colourful *kanga* wraps sell sweetened *mandazi* bread, fried and scented with cardamom. Although its history lies in a blend of distinct culinary traditions – Indian, Arabian and Bantu African – Swahili cooking has a distinct identity in its own right, with unique flavours and improvisations, special dishes for celebrations and quick roadside snacks.

At the break of dawn, as fishermen board their *dhow* boats and sail out into open waters, women boil sweet milky tea, often flavoured with a masala spice mixture of black pepper, cinnamon and cardamom. *Uji* porridge made from ground maize is served in shallow bowls as the day's work begins. Although food stalls selling roasted cassava roots, chapati and fried bread opens in the late morning, the midday meal is not taken until well into the afternoon. Even then, it is usually a simple affair of cooked *wali* rice and *maharagwe* bean stew with vegetables, often followed by a short rest during the heat of the day, after which work begins again.

Main meals are usually eaten at home, but in the larger villages and towns roadside stalls and kiosks sell snacks and quick meals for workers and passers-by. Juice vendors squeeze sugar cane stalks through a hand-operated press and customers stop for a glass, drinking while they gather around the vendor in the open street. Night markets, the most famous of which takes place in Forodhani Gardens in Zanzibar's Stone Town, are a popular treat. Families and groups of young people wander the stalls where fresh seafood, fish, samosa and chapati cook over blazing charcoal grills. Slices of ruby-coloured watermelons and glasses of fresh juice conclude the meal, which is eaten standing up or on benches placed behind stalls near the sea. Cassava chips, flavoured with lime juice and chilli powder, are sold by the bag and vendors compete in volume and extravagance to attract hungry patrons to their stalls.

In the traditional stone houses of the old towns, the kitchen is located on the rooftop of the house and accessed by special stairway from the courtyard on the first floor. In village houses, women cook outside their homes, seated on woven *mkeka* mats where the open air, easy ventilation and shared company make food preparation a joyous and sociable event. Every Swahili kitchen has a *jiko* stove and a bag of charcoal, or *mkaa*, to heat it. So important is this portable stove that the Swahili word for kitchen, *jikoni*, literally translates into 'by the *jiko.*' Fresh water, in villages drawn from a communal tap or well, is stored at home in covered clay pots called *mtungi* set upon metal stands. Aluminium saucepans called *sufuria* are stirred with hand-carved wooden spoons, and soup or *mchuzi* stew is ladled into hollowed-out coconut shells attached to long sticks. A small folding stool with a serrated blade on one end, called an *mbuzi*, is used for grating coconut – a daily chore for women along the coast, where so many dishes centre around this life-giving tree. Fresh coconut milk is squeezed from a *kifumbu*, a hollow cylinder made from palm fronds woven into *mkeka*. Dried beans and uncooked rice are stored in *mkeka* baskets called *kikapu*, which also double as shopping baskets and storage containers around the house.

Swahili families live together within towns or villages and shopping is a daily affair, a chance for women to meet each other in the *sokoni* market, exchange news and chat. In the small fishing villages that dot the coast, market day occurs about twice a week, when the women of the area come together to sell their wares in the shade and catch up on local events. Larger towns have a central market that opens daily from early morning, when

vendors arrive with *kikapu* baskets brimming with fresh produce picked from their shamba farms that dawn – mounds of ruby red tomatoes, dark purple onions, spiky pineapples and plenty of ripe mangoes sold by the basketful. In the villages small *duka* shops sell basic supplies and fresh produce, but in the stone towns individual stalls specialise in freshly ground spices, lentils and rice or live chickens and fresh eggs. The larger *sokoni* all have special corners dedicated to fish and seafood – shaded markets where fishermen arrive in the morning and evening to sell their catches fresh from the Indian Ocean. Bright-eyed tuna and tender octopus, translucent prawns as long as a man's hand and local *changu* fish are all for sale at a negotiable price. Small minnows hang suspended on wires in the sun to make dried fish *dagaa*, a staple of the working man's diet.

Many basic dishes form the basis of main meals along the Swahili Coast and all of them can be added to and embellished for special occasions. The most popular main dish is indubitably *mchuzi*, a thick spiced stew of fish, seafood, meat or vegetables. *Mchuzi* is best served with cooked rice infused with coconut or a fresh *chapati* browned slightly on both sides. Seafood or fish *mchuzi* forms the foundation of most meals and vegetables are often added to the stew to thicken its consistency and add flavour. Spices continue to play an incredibly important part in Swahili cooking, a legacy of Indian and Arabian influences brought to the coast centuries ago. Cinnamon, cloves, cardamom and ginger form the basis of many sweet dishes and drinks and are grown in abundance on the islands of Zanzibar. Whole spices are ground by hand just before cooking on a *jiwe la kusaga dawa*, an oblong mortar stone.

For centuries, rich merchants living in Swahili towns have owned plantations called *konde* located within travelling distance of their grand stone houses. Every wealthy Swahili merchant and aristocrat had his own town home and a country plantation to provide for the needs of his large household. The *konde* were tropical paradises of mango and cloves planted in ordered lines, thick banana groves, a profusion of local vegetables and towering avocado and tamarind trees. The country plantations also functioned as private retreats for the ruling classes. In her autobiography *Memoirs of an Arabian Princess from Zanzibar*, Princess Salme writes of spending long weeks on the *konde* with her family, and of the preparations and excitement with which the journey was anticipated.

Some of the ingredients and methods in Swahili cooking are rather foreign in the western kitchen. Coconut is used extensively in savoury dishes and ingredients such as tamarind and plantains require some daring to prepare for the first time. The effort is more than worth it and whether you're cooking for a large dinner party or a romantic meal for two, we hope that you will find the following recipes as enjoyable to prepare as they are to eat. As we say in Swahili, *karibu chakula*. Welcome to our food.

Below are some of common ingredients in Swahili cooking that may require some extra preparation:

Bananas and plantains: Bananas grow in abundance all over the Swahili Coast, from sweet finger-sized bunches to long stalks of starchy plantains. You can buy plantains from ethnic supermarkets and their shelf life is considerably longer than what sweet bananas. Many of the plantain dishes in this book require cooking the bananas with their skins on, so be sure to read the directions carefully before starting.

Calamari: Calamari or squid is incredibly versatile and easy to prepare. To avoid the rubbery texture often associated with it, cook the calamari either very quickly over a high flame or very slowly – at least 45 minutes – over low heat. Buy it ready-prepared or have your fishmonger clean it for you. If you've bought a whole calamari, on your hands, soak it in cold water for 30 minutes. Holding the sac in one hand and the tentacles in the other, pull gently so that the tentacles separate from the body. Cut them straight across, just above the eyes, and throw away everything from the eyes down. Make sure you squeeze off the small beak at the bottom of the tentacles. If your calamari is particularly large, try to remove as much of the skin as you can before rinsing everything in cold water, patting it dry and proceeding.

Coconut: *Nazi*, as it is known on the East African coast, is one of the most important ingredients in Swahili cooking. Coconut milk is squeezed by hand through a woven *mkeka* cylinder called a *kifumbo* and the flesh is grated on a stool called an *mbuzi*, which has a sharp serrated blade attached to one end. For the recipes in this book, canned or powdered coconut milk is a sufficient stand-in for fresh coconut milk, and if you don't own a good grater, desiccated coconut works just as well.

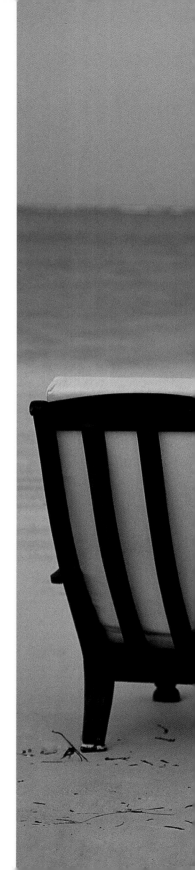

Octopus: Called *pweza* in Kiswahili, octopus is a main staple of *mchuzi* stews and popular village food all over the Swahili Coast. When buying your octopus, make sure it has been well tenderised, otherwise the flesh will be totally inedible. Village women do this by banging the creature on coral rocks, but should you have doubts, a large mallet will do.

Prawns: When buying prawns it is very important that they are of the freshest possible quality – their flesh should be shiny and translucent. Before cooking them, gently remove their heads and make sure that no residue remains. If they are to be served peeled, remove the shells and with a sharp knife and cut along their backbone to remove the dark spine.

Tamarind: Tamarind is one of the most delectable and unique flavours in Swahili cooking, and packaged blocks of tamarind pulp are now readily available in ethnic supermarkets. Its sweet and sour bite adds an element much like lemon juice or vinegar in western cooking. Known as *mkwaju* in Swahili, the tamarind pod grows on a towering tree with umbrella-like branches. To prepare the pulp for a recipe, pour hot water over the dry fruit and leave it to set, later squeezing through a sieve to produce the cooking liquid.

All recipes serve four people.

Lamu

*Ahodha wengi, chombo
huenda mrama.
Too many cooks spoil
the broth.*

Tusitiri Dhow

There are thousands of islands in the Lamu Archipelago and Tusitiri Dhow – a grand *jahazi* in the style of the old Swahili traders – perfectly recaptures what life in the archipelago was like so many centuries ago. Island-hopping from Lamu to Kiwayu Island, the 20-metre wooden sailing boat is about as romantic a means of transportation as you're likely to find. With her full cream-coloured sails and polished mahogany floors, the boat is as timelessly elegant as it is unerringly traditional. Tusitiri, whose name means 'something we treasure' in Swahili, is the ultimate Indian Ocean safari in decadent Swahili style.

Sailing through Dodori Creek and all the isolated inlets, abandoned islands and wide waters in between, Tusitiri Dhow takes full advantage of the bounty of the Indian Ocean. Whether enjoying a three-course lunch while moored off a lush stretch of desert beach, game-viewing along the mainland coast or rocking gently over a quiet coral bay, mealtimes on Tusitiri are memorable affairs. As the wooden *jahazi* plies the bright waters of the Indian Ocean, guests are treated to a gourmet spread of plentiful seafood and fish, often so fresh it spends only hours between the water and the serving plate.

Meals are served around a hardwood table shaded by the high mast and a full sail extends above the deck in waves of sparkling white canvas. In the morning, a spread of fresh fruits – ripe mangoes, bright orange papayas and star-shaped pineapple slices – awaits early risers as the sun climbs over the horizon. After a morning spent fishing off the *dhow*, scuba-diving an undiscovered reef or just lounging on the mats and pillows piled abundantly on deck, a five-course lunch cooked on the boat's open-air kitchen is served around the central table. By the time night falls, the scene is set for an intimate night under the African stars. Dinner is an all-evening affair of course after course, all based around the freshest ingredients the archipelago has to offer. Tusitiri's menus are a creative mix of Swahili specialities, Asian flavours and Italian dishes – a dextrous variety of cuisine and flavours.

Coconut Fish Soup with Saffron
Crab Cocktail with Crushed Peanuts
Fish in Sambal with Vegetables in a Coconut Shell
Caramel Bananas with Tamarind Syrup

Coconut Fish Soup with Saffron

This classic fish soup is made more exotic with the addition of saffron, a prized ingredient from the bazaars of Persia. Although powdered saffron can be used in this recipe, if you have real saffron threads add a few for an authentic touch.

Ingredients

4 cups fish stock
2 cups coconut milk
6 tomatoes, peeled and chopped
1 medium onion, sliced
3 cloves of garlic, peeled and crushed
1 teaspoon saffron powder or a few saffron threads
2 teaspoons fresh coriander, chopped
salt and pepper to taste

Place the oil in a saucepan, add the garlic and sauté for 5 minutes. Add the sliced onion and the saffron and sauté, stirring frequently, until the onions are soft. Add the tomatoes and one cup of the coconut milk and cook over medium heat for 10 minutes. Add the remaining coconut milk and the fish stock, and simmer covered for another 30 minutes. Season to taste, add the chopped coriander, and serve.

Crab Cocktail with Crushed Peanuts

Crushed peanuts give this seafood cocktail an element of the Far East, accentuated with the addition of lime juice, coriander and peanut oil. Leftover crab meat is perfect for this starter. Otherwise, make sure to boil the crab meat well before adding the other ingredients.

Ingredients

I cup crab meat, cooked
2 cloves of garlic, crushed
3 teaspoons lime juice
2 teaspoons peanut oil
1/2 cup roasted peanuts, peeled and crushed
1 avocado, peeled
1 teaspoon fresh coriander, chopped

In a mixing bowl, combine the crab, garlic, lime juice, peanut oil and coriander. Slice the avocado across the centre so that each piece forms a complete ring – a medium sized avocado should yield about 4 slices. Place each ring on a serving plate and spoon the crab mixture into the middle. Sprinkle with crushed peanuts and serve.

Preheat an oven to 180°C. Mix all the ingredients – except for the fish fillets – in a bowl. Place each fillet on a square of aluminium foil and spread 1 tablespoon of the coconut sambal over it, wrapping in the foil to form small parcels. Bake for 20 minutes and serve topped with the remaining sambal.

To make the vegetables, make sure the oven is still heated to 180°C. Gently sauté the garlic and ginger in the vegetable oil. Add the pumpkin and sweet potato cubes and sauté for 10 minutes. Add the spinach and sauté for another 5 minutes, then divide the vegetables between the coconut shells and fill each one to the brim. Sprinkle with bread crumbs and drizzle with peanut oil. Bake for 15 minutes, then serve.

Fish in Sambal with Vegetables in a Coconut Shell

Using a coconut shell as a container for serving vegetables adds a creative element to the table and the soft coconut flesh makes a savoury accompaniment to sweet potatoes, pumpkin, and spinach.

Ingredients

4 fish fillets, preferably red snapper, 250 g each

1 cup grated coconut

1 onion, chopped

2 teaspoons lime juice

1 teaspoon fresh coriander, chopped

1 green chilli, minced

for the vegetables

4 coconuts, their tops hacked off

1 cup pumpkin, chopped into 2-cm cubes

1cup sweet potatoes, chopped into 2-cm cubes

2 large handfuls of spinach, washed and finely chopped

1-cm piece of ginger, minced

2 cloves of garlic

1 tablespoon vegetable oil

1 tablespoon bread crumbs

4 tablespoons peanut oil

Caramel Bananas with Tamarind Syrup

Sweet and sticky bananas are made slightly sour with the addition of thick tamarind syrup, made from pods off the towering *mkwaju* tree. This eye-catching dessert is perfect for a special occasion.

Ingredients

4 large bananas

2 tablespoons vegetable oil

1 egg and 1 egg white
2 tablespoons flour
2 tablespoons yoghurt
2 tablespoons milk
6 tablespoons sugar
4 tablespoons water for the tamarind syrup
3 teaspoons tamarind liquid
4 teaspoons sugar
1 tablespoon golden syrup
500 ml water

Whisk the egg whites until stiff and set aside. In another bowl, whisk together the whole egg, milk, yogurt and flour. With a wooden spoon, gently fold in the whisked egg whites. Heat the oil in a frying pan until smoking hot. Cut the bananas into 2-cm chunks and dip each banana into the egg and flour batter to coat well. Fry a few at a time until the bananas are golden brown on both sides, then remove with a slotted spoon and drain on absorbent paper. While you fry them in batches, keep the cooked bananas warm under oiled aluminium foil.

To make the caramel topping, heat the sugar and water in a heavy saucepan until the sugar has dissolved. Boil the syrup rapidly until the sugar forms a soft ball when tested in a glass of cold water. Make sure you do not boil beyond this point – the syrup will become too hard. Remove the pan from the heat and place it in a bowl of cold water. Dip a spoon into the syrup and slowly pull the spoon upwards until it forms thin strings. Twist the strings over the bananas and repeat until most of the syrup has been used up.

To make the tamarind syrup, combine all the ingredients in a saucepan and bring to the boil. Simmer gently over low heat for 20 minutes or until the sauce has been reduced by half and thickens to a syrupy consistency. Top the caramel fried bananas with tamarind syrup and serve.

Kijani House Hotel

In the lush gardens and terraces of Kijani House Hotel, the Swahili spirit is alive and well. As the call to prayer is chanted out from Shela Village's Friday Mosque and echoes from the rooftops, the rhythm of rest and work, food and refreshment is carried on within its walls. From small swimming pools glistening in the broken shadows of flowering frangipani, flamboyant and palm trees to the antique furnishings and ornaments in each cool and shaded room, Kijani House Hotel offers guests the opportunity to relax and unwind in authentic surroundings. Meals at Kijani are refined experiences in good living and fine taste. Ornately carved furniture and hanging Arab lanterns add to the atmosphere of secluded Swahili living. Laid-back and informal courses of carefully prepared food tempt the eye and the appetite. The property's food is a blend of classic elements of the best Italian and French cooking, fresh ingredients and the array of spices available around Lamu.

Pierre Oberson and his wife Mwanashee are firmly committed to the Swahili value of self-sufficiency and absolute freshness – principles which translate into brilliant dishes and piquant flavours. Traditionally, the families of Lamu and the Swahili Coast attempted to grow and produce everything themselves – in such isolated surroundings, it could be weeks or months until the next supply ship arrived. In the past, wealthy merchants and landowners had family plantations called *konde* on the surrounding islands, where their labourers farmed tropical fruits and local vegetables and cared for poultry and sometimes small herds of cattle and goats. Kijani also has such a plantation, and often the food on a guest's plate has come directly from the farm – ripe mangoes, soft papayas, passion fruit, limes, melons, coconut and cashew nuts all arrive daily, fresh from the fields. Eggs come in small crates by boat and the milk arrives by donkey-back early in the morning. Home-made marmalade, ice-cream and bread are daily staple at Kijani House – with food so fresh and ripened by the tropical sun, the flavours are simple and strong.

Oriental Tuna Carpaccio
Black Ink Risotto 'Manda Toto'
Saffron Fish Pot 'Valparaiso'
Grilled Pineapple and Mango with Tamarind Ice Cream

Oriental Tuna Carpaccio

This is an incredibly simple yet elegant recipe, but make sure you use only the freshest fish. To keep the dish cool, refrigerate your serving plates before assembling. Carpaccio is wonderful served with toast and butter, or even with a light mix of freshly grated horseradish and fresh cream.

Ingredients

400 g tuna fillets, frozen for at least 3 hours

2 teaspoons olive oil

1 teaspoon soy sauce

1 teaspoon fish sauce

1 teaspoon grated ginger

2 teaspoons lime juice or 1 teaspoon rice vinegar

1 teaspoon white pepper

1 teaspoon lime zest

1 cup sesame oil

avocado slices and tomato cubes, to garnish

Mix all the ingredients except the tuna in a small bowl until everything is well blended. With a very sharp knife, slice the frozen tuna as thin as you possibly can and arrange them on your serving plates. Sprinkle the dressing over them and refrigerate for another 10 minutes.

Black Ink Risotto 'Manda Toto'

This classic Italian risotto is best made with an Italian rice like arborio, carnaroli or vialone, which all have round, almost spherical shapes and a creamy texture when cooked. The risotto is done when the rice is soft on the outside and a bit hard on the inside – al dente, just like pasta.

Ingredients

2 cups arborio rice

1.5 litres fish stock

1.5 litres chicken stock

1 onion, chopped

2 cloves garlic, chopped

3 teaspoons olive oil

2 teaspoons butter

200 ml white wine

250 g calamari, cut into slices

50 ml squid ink

4 king prawns, to garnish

1 tomato, diced, to garnish

1 handful chopped dill or parsley, to garnish

Mix the fish and chicken stock together and put half of it in a large saucepan, reserving the rest for later. Boil the calamari and prawns in half the stock until tender, drain, and aside. In the same saucepan, heat the olive oil and half the butter. Add the onion, garlic and rice and stir gently with a wooden spoon for about 3 minutes or until the rice is transparent – this means it has soaked up the seasoning. Add the white wine and ladle by ladle over low heat, add the rest of the hot stock, waiting until the rice has absorbed each ladleful before adding more. Make sure you stir slowly and thoroughly the whole time. After the rice has been cooking for 5 minutes, add the squid ink and stir for another 10 minutes. When the rice is just starting to soften but is still al dente, add the boiled calamari and 3 minutes later, the butter. Serve garnished with the boiled prawns, herbs and tomatoes.

Saffron Fish Pot 'Valparaiso'

This warming meal is as nourishing as it is comforting — fragrant, saffron-infused rice with hunks of seafood and fresh fish.

Ingredients

2 litres fish stock

1 cup arborio rice

200 ml dry white wine

1 pinch ground saffron

1 pinch saffron threads, soaked in the white wine

500 g assorted vegetables (carrots, celery, green pepper and fennel), chopped

600 g mixed seafood (prawns, mussels or calamari), cut into pieces

300g fish, cut into 2-cm by 2-cm cubes

a pinch of fresh dill, celery leaves or fennel greens, to garnish

salt and freshly ground black pepper

In a large saucepan, bring the fish stock to the boil and add the vegetables, rice and saffron powder. Simmer uncovered on medium heat for about 10 minutes, stirring regularly. About 10 minutes before the rice is ready, when it's just starting to soften, add the seafood and about 5 minutes later, the fish. When the rice is cooked but still al dente, add the white wine and soaked saffron, stir to mix, and serve.

Grilled Pineapple and Mango with Tamarind Ice Cream

This recipe is worth making just for the taste of cardamom-scented pineapple marinated in port and sugar, crystallised gently on the grill. Tamarind makes a delightfully refreshing ice cream and a cool complement to this very special dessert.

Ingredients

1 pineapple

1 large mango or 2 small ones, pureed

200 ml water

100 ml port

3 teaspoons sugar

10 cardamom pods, lightly crushed

1 teaspoon butter

2 teaspoons honey for the ice cream

4 egg yolks

140 g sugar

300 ml milk

1 vanilla pod or 1 teaspoon vanilla essence

120 ml tamarind puree

300 ml double cream

Make the ice cream first. Whisk the yolks and sugar together until they double in volume. In a large saucepan, bring the milk almost to the boil and add the vanilla. Add a cupful of the milk to the yolk mixture and stir to mix. Turn the heat to low and make sure the mixture doesn't boil or it will curdle. Add the yolk mixture to the hot milk and vanilla, stirring constantly. When the mixture has thickened, or after you have been stirring for about 3 minutes, remove the custard from the heat and add the tamarind puree and cream. Follow the directions for your ice cream maker or pour the mixture into a plastic container and place in the freezer, removing it every

15 minutes to beat thoroughly until well frozen.

In a large saucepan, bring the water, port, sugar and cardamom to the boil and let it simmer on medium heat for 5 minutes. Cool slightly, strain and place in a plastic container. Slice the pineapple and cut each slice into 6 sections. Add the pineapple to the syrup and refrigerate for 1-2 hours. Drain the pineapple and mash the remaining syrup with the mango to make a thick cream. Place the pineapple on skewers and grill them gently for a few minutes on each side, taking care they don't burn. Let them cool for 10 minutes, sieve, and place in a plastic container. Slice the pineapple and divide the slices into 6 sections. Add the pineapple to the syrup and refrigerate for 1-2 hours. Drain the pineapple and mash the remaining syrup with the mango to make a thick cream. Place the pineapple on skewers and grill them gently for a few minutes on each side, taking care they don't burn.

To serve, place a few pieces of pineapple over a dollop of mango cream and serve with the tamarind ice cream.

Peponi Hotel

Peponi Hotel's world-class reputation has made it a favourite for visitors to the archipelago. On the residents' balcony just over the bustling waterfront, stately white columns and large windows add a sense of colonial grandeur to the Swahili grounds. Around the bar and courtyard, simple decor mixes with classic maritime themes – nautical maps and sailing instruments, *dhow eyes* and handmade miniatures of the many *dhow* boats outside. In the gardens that surround the elegant rooms, winding stairways lead to sheltered rooftops where *kikoi*-covered swings overlook the sandy beach just below.

Peponi Hotel's classic food and elegant surroundings make dinner a special occasion for hotel guests and the ex-pat residents alike. The experience of dinner at Peponi definitely starts in the colonial-style bar, an irresistibly social spot at any time of day that really comes alive after sunset. Lamu aficionados, Shela resident and hotel guests share well-mixed cocktails and hot snacks of fried oysters and spiced fish over conversations of the day's adventures. Soon, a three-course dinner is served on the airy balcony or beside a tall wall of niched *zidaka*.

Peponi Hotel offers classic continental dishes, but their Swahili cooking is a special favourite. A full-course Swahili menu is on offer every evening – an authentic sampling of the best seafood dishes and local specialities of the coast. Plates of hot *bhajia* and spiced *samosa* arrive with dipping sauce. *Samaki wa kupaka* – whole grilled fish in cumin, pepper, cinnamon, tamarind and coconut cream – or prawns *mchuzi* arrive at the table smelling of freshly ground spices. Plates of spinach in coconut milk, green lentils called *pojo* cooked in spices and the classic African *maharagwe* beans come with steaming bowls of coconut rice and plates of hot *chapatis*. Traditional Swahili coffee is served in tall braziers, the thick brew simmering with cardamom and sugar, accompanied by small pieces of dark *halua*, a sticky confection flavoured with rose water in the Arabian tradition. Peponi even serves a Swahili breakfast of fresh tropical fruit, savoury *mbaazi* pulses in coconut cream, spiced doughnuts called *mahamri* and tall cups of sweet masala *chai* flavoured with cloves, cinnamon, ginger and black pepper.

Old Pal Cocktail
Spicy Mango Soup
Mchuzi na Kamba
Ginger Nut Lime Pie

Old Pal Cocktail

Lime juice and angostura bitters add a refreshing edge to this sundown cocktail, making it the perfect close to a long day in the sun. To make your drink extra cold, freeze the vodka and your glass and chill the lime juice before serving.

Ingredients (per drink)
1 tablespoon sugar
2 tots of vodka
a few drops of angostura bitters
1 tot of fresh lime juice, but keep the limes
soda water
crushed ice

Rub one of the cut limes around the rim of a tall glass and dip it into white sugar. Add crushed ice to almost fill the glass and pour over a few sparing drops of angostura bitters. Add the vodka and lime juice, top up with soda water and serve.

Spicy Mango Soup

This hot soup combines the tropical flavours of coconut and mango – a perfect palate-teaser. For best results, use apple mangoes, as other varieties tend to be quite pithy.

Ingredients
15 g butter
2 tablespoons olive oil
2 onions, chopped
2 cloves of garlic, chopped
1 teaspoon fresh ginger, grated
1 chilli or a few dashes of chilli sauce
1 small sprig fresh rosemary or 1 teaspoon dried and powdered
2 unripe, slightly green mangoes
1 cup coconut cream
1.5 litres chicken stock

Sauté the onions with the butter and oil until they are golden and translucent. Add the garlic, ginger and the rosemary and continue to sauté until fragrant. Then add the chopped mango and cook for another two or three minutes until everything is soft. Ladle in the chicken stock and simmer for 15 to 20 minutes or until the mango is starting to disintegrate. Remove from the heat and discard the fresh rosemary. Puree the soup in a blender and if the mangoes are still stringy, push them through a sieve. Season to taste and right before serving, stir in the coconut cream.

Mchuzi na Kamba

In Swahili, *mchuzi* is a spicy stew or curry made from a base of meat, seafood or vegetables. It forms the base of the main evening meal and is usually served with *chapati* or coconut rice.

Ingredients
1.5 kg king prawns, cleaned and peeled
4 tablespoons vegetable oil
1 litre coconut cream
8 garlic of cloves, chopped

4 onions, chopped
4 teaspoons ground cinnamon
75 g tamarind pulp
8 tomatoes, peeled and chopped
2 tablespoons tomato paste
2 teaspoons ground cardamom
chopped fresh coriander to garnish

Place the tamarind pulp in a small bowl and pour 8 tablespoons of boiling water over it. Mash gently with a spoon and set aside. Put the onion and garlic in a mortar and pestle or a food processor and crush them together until the mixture becomes thick paste. Slowly add the tomatoes and continue to mix.

In a frying pan, heat the oil and add the onion paste. Cook, stirring frequently, for 5 minutes. Strain the tamarind juice and slowly add it to the onion paste. Simmer for 3 minutes. Add the prawns to the sauce and sauté until pink and firm, for about 7-10 minutes. Lower the heat and add the coconut cream. Mix well and remove from the heat. Garnish with fresh coriander and serve.

Ginger Nut Lime Pie

A Swahili version of a classic favourite, this pie combines the orchard-grown limes of Lamu with ginger, a traditional Swahili digestive. The pie can be made in advance, but if your refrigerator is very cold you might want to remove it and let it soften a few minutes before serving.

Ingredients
500 g ginger biscuits
250 g butter
4 eggs
2 tins of evaporated milk, 800 ml each
1/2 cup lime juice
200 g sugar
2 teaspoons lime zest
whipped cream, whole fresh strawberries and slices of lime to garnish.

To make the crust, mash the biscuits into a fine powder by putting them in a plastic bag and crunching well with a rolling pin, or pulverising them in a food processor. Melt the butter in a saucepan and add the powdered biscuits. When well mixed, press the mixture evenly into a 30-cm pie dish and refrigerate.

To make the filling, separate the eggs and whisk the yolks and sugar until the mixture is white and frothy. Add the evaporated milk and continue whisking, then add the lime juice and zest. Beat everything until light and well blended. In a separate bowl, whisk the egg whites until they form stiff peaks, the fold them into the milk mixture. Pour the filling into the refrigerated crust and return everything to the refrigerator and chill at least 3 hours before serving. Decorate with whipped cream, strawberry halves and twists of lime.

Beach House

The kitchen at Beach House is wide and spacious, full of light and the sounds of the narrow streets just outside. True to the concept of the Swahili kitchen, the chef cooks only what is available seasonally on the island – a commitment that produces incredible variety with the changing of the seasons and the coming of the monsoon rains. An Italian influence pervades the kitchen and the fusion of European favourites and local tastes gives the food a fresh and creative flavour.

Beach House caters for groups of family and friends on short or extended stays, so chefs work around the availability of ingredients and guests' personal preferences. Every morning, fishermen come to the kitchen doors of the houses to sell their catch – fresh crabs still scuttling in their cages, lobsters extending tentative antenna outside their box and fish glistening and fresh from the sea. Women travel from their garden *shambas* with woven baskets called *kikapu* full to the brim with sun-ripened mangoes and golden papayas, crisp green peppers and juicy tomatoes. The vendors sell their produce directly to the houses' chefs for use in the kitchen that day and often ingredients spend only hours between the garden and the serving plate.

In the kitchen, the emphasis is on home-made food fresh from the garden and the sea. Bread, muffins, marmalades, chutneys, ice cream and sorbets emerge from the kitchens daily. Breakfast is an informal affair of fresh fruit, home-made muesli, juices and hot drinks. Lunch is often light fish cerviche, carpaccio, cold seafood and plenty of fresh salads on offer in the open dining room, on the acacia-shaded terrace, up on the roof or even as a picnic lunch on the beach. Dinner starts with sundowners on the rooftop surrounded by the old town of Shela and the waterfront, followed by a procession of soups and salads, seafood and light dishes flavoured with coconut and Swahili spices.

Watermelon Cooler
Prawns and Avocado Salad with Mango
Cold Lobster in Coconut Sauce
Passion Fruit Sorbet

Watermelon Cooler

It's important to use fresh fruits for this eye-catching cooler — the taste of freshly squeezed citrus brings out the gentle flavour of the watermelon. This iced refresher is a perfect pick-me-up after a morning in the sun. For an evening treat, add a shot of chilled vodka to each glass.

Ingredients
1 medium-size watermelon
1 cup orange juice, preferably fresh
1/4 cup lime or lemon juice, freshly squeezed
sugar to taste
crushed ice

Cut the watermelon open and with a large spoon, remove all the pulp from the inside and put it in a large bowl. Pass the fruit through a sieve and stir it to remove the pips. For every 4 parts of watermelon, add 1 part orange juice and 1 part lime or lemon juice. Try a spoonful of the mixture at this point and add sugar to taste. Serve the watermelon cooler in tall glasses topped with crushed ice.

Prawns and Avocado Salad with Mango

This salad takes full advantage of the plentiful mangoes and avocados that grow along the Swahili Coast — the dark waxy leaves of mango and avocado trees are a common sight in villagers' *shamba* farms. Bacon can be substituted for shrimp in this colourful cold salad.

Ingredients
500g king prawns
2 mangoes

2 medium-sized avocados

a squeeze of lemon juice

4 tablespoons olive oil

1 tablespoon white wine vinegar

salt and black pepper

fresh coriander to garnish

Boil the king prawns for five minutes and drain them in a colander. When they've cooled a bit, peel them with a sharp knife to remove their crustaceous shell. Clean them by removing the sticky yellow substance around their feet and remove their heads. Using a sharp knife, slit along the backs of the prawns and remove the black vein. Put them in a bowl, cover and refrigerate.

Cut the mangoes into cubes by splitting them in half on either side of the seed. Make criss-cross cuts across each side with a sharp knife, and turn each half inside out and slice the squares from the skin. Cut the avocados in half and remove the seed, making sure that none of the brown-paper like covering sticks to the fruit. Like you did with the mango, cut vertical slices through the fruit against the skin, turn the avocado half inside out and slice the fruit off. Squeeze a little lemon over the avocado to prevent it from discolouring. Put the mango cubes and the avocado slices in the bowl with the prawns and leave them inside the fridge for now.

In a large serving bowl, mix the olive oil, white wine vinegar, salt and freshly ground black pepper until everything is well combined. Tip in the bowl of prawns, mango, and avocado and toss until the dressing coats everything well. Chop some fresh coriander to sprinkle over the salad.

Fill a large bucket with ice water and plunge in the live lobsters. Cover, leave the room, and come back 30 minutes later. Fill a large pot with heavily salted water and bring it to a boil, then add the lobsters and cook them 12-15 minutes per 500g lobster, then 10 additional minutes for each 500g. Drain and let cool. Cut the lobster in half horizontally, open the shell and clean. Put the lobster meat in a bowl, cover and refrigerate it until later.

Heat the olive oil in a large, heavy-bottomed pan. Add the onions and green peppers and fry them over medium heat for about 5 minutes, until the onions are translucent and beginning to colour and the green peppers are soft and fragrant. Add the chopped tomatoes and let the mixture simmer for another 5 minutes, stirring regularly. When the tomatoes have released their juices and the mixture resembles a sauce, add the tomato paste, coconut milk and curry powder. Season to taste. Remove the sauce from the heat and let it cool. Before serving, arrange the lobster on a plate and pour the sauce over the meat.

Cold Lobster with Coconut Sauce

Coconut milk is readily available on the Swahili Coast, where each woman grates her own on an *mbuzi*, a low bench with a blade attached to the end that scrapes the fruit out of its hard shell. This dish makes a refreshing addition to a summer picnic – for an authentic Swahili meal, serve it with *pilau* or coconut rice.

Ingredients

1 kg live lobsters

salted water

2 small onions, finely chopped

4 cloves of garlic, squeezed through a press or finely chopped

2 small green peppers, finely chopped

2 tomatoes, finely chopped

2 teaspoons tomato paste

250 ml coconut milk, prepared and ready to use

2 teaspoons of curry powder

salt and pepper

Passion Fruit Sorbet

Passion fruit lends this sorbet a slightly astringent and sour taste that is the perfect palate-cleanser to a summer meal. If you're using an ice-cream machine, follow the manufacturer's instructions to freeze the syrup but if you don't, you can easily do this by hand. Just make sure you have a large plastic container with as much surface area as possible – the more surface is exposed, the better the sorbet will freeze.

Ingredients

250 ml water

250 g sugar

500 ml passion pulp (about 12 medium-sized fruits)

optional vodka

Put the water and sugar into a heavy pot over low heat. As the mixture heats up, stir the sugar until you see that it's dissolved completely and there are no granules visible. Remove from the heat and let the syrup cool.

In the meantime, cut the passion fruits in half and scoop the pulp into a blender or food processor with a spoon. Blend the fruit with a little bit of water and strain the mixture to remove the seeds. Mix the passion pulp with the cooled syrup until the two are well blended.

If you have an ice-cream maker, follow the manufacturer's instructions for making sorbet. If not, find the largest shallow plastic container you have and pour the passion syrup in. Put the mixture in your freezer and every 15 minutes, stir with a metal spoon so that the ice crystals come to the middle. After about 2 hours, the mixture will be frozen. This sorbet freezes hard, so about 15 minutes before serving, remove it from the freezer and let it soften. Serve either on its own or with a shot of vodka. The astringent taste of the vodka complements the citrus-like sweetness of the passion fruit perfectly.

Fatuma's Tower

Named after a mysterious Swahili woman who lived unmarried and alone on the property more than a century ago, Fatuma's Tower is now dedicated wholly to the body and soul. The only yoga retreat in the whole of Kenya, Fatuma's Tower is a haven of simple living and natural style. Pomegranates and tamarind trees grow in abundance within the walled garden, and in the evening night jasmine scents the air with hints of the orient. A shaded *baraza* area is the perfect place for afternoon tea or freshly squeezed juice before an hour-long yoga session. An umbrella-shaped acacia tree shades the cushions and planter's chairs, dropping its small yellow flowers on the sand. Birds and cicadas call and chirrup through the evening as the tower lights up, casting a light glow around the property as night falls.

Little is known about the proprietress of the original Swahili house whose ruins, overcome by palm trees and flowering vines, make up a central feature of the entranceway. The central tower dates back more than 300 years, but the entire structure was abandoned after Fatuma's death and was left in ruins for almost a century. The yoga hall retains some of the original plasterwork of the old house, which has been rebuilt beside the original ruins, and the decor remains staunchly Swahili in its simplicity and design.

The food at Fatuma's Tower is natural and fresh vegetarian fare served with plenty of Swahili spices and seafood dishes cooked in traditional style. Dining takes place in a small courtyard in the centre of the property, its corners filled with a collection of antiques from India and the Kenyan coast. Across from the long table, an ancient tamarind tree whose branches reach the top of the old tower offers welcome shade from the midday sun. Under an outlying staircase that leads to the yoga hall and upstairs rooms, a Swahili bench inlaid with Indian tiles stands under a collection of antique *dhow* eyes. Hand-blown glass buoys in greens and blues lie on the ground between paving tiles imprinted with the silhouettes of fish and sea turtles.

Tamarind Juice
Bhajia with Tamarind Sauce
Fish Pilau with Coconut Mchicha
Swahili Puddini

Tamarind Juice

The *mkwaju*, as the tamarind tree is called in Swahili, makes an impressive sight, its dark pods hanging like ornaments from the elegant branches. Lamu is famous for its juices and Fatuma's Tower, with its emphasis on fresh and healthy food, makes jugs of tamarind juice every morning. Lucky for them, a tamarind tree grows in the central courtyard and fresh tamarind pods are always on hand.

Ingredients
200 g tamarind pulp
250 g sugar
2 litres water

Put the tamarind pulp in a large bowl. Bring the water and the sugar to the boil and simmer until the sugar has dissolved. Pour the syrup over the tamarind pods and use a wooden spoon to break up the pulp. Let set until cool, about 30 minutes, and strain into a jug. Chill before serving.

Bhajia with Tamarind Sauce

Bhajia are a popular Indian snack that has become a favourite along the Swahili Coast. In large towns, snack stands sell freshly fried balls of spiced potatoes or lentils coated in batter and steaming to the touch.

Ingredients
500 g green lentils, soaked for 3 hours
2 onions, chopped
2 cloves of garlic, minced
1 green chilli, minced
1 handful of fresh coriander, chopped
vegetable oil for frying
for the tamarind sauce
75 g tamarind
150 ml water
1/2 teaspoon chilli powder
1 clove of garlic, minced

To make the tamarind sauce, boil the water and pour it over the tamarind pulp. Let stand for 15 minutes, sieve and mix the liquid with chilli powder and garlic.
Clean the lentils to make sure there are no stones and pulse them in a food processor until finely grated but not minced. Mix in the onions, garlic, chilli, fresh coriander and salt to taste. Mould into small flat cakes. Heat the oil in a deep frying pan until it splutters when you add a few drops of water. Fry the bhajia, a few at a time, until they are golden brown on both sides.

Fish Pilau served with Coconut Mchicha

Pilau is a traditional dish of rice cooked with whole spices. Fish is often added to make the meal more of a special occasion. The best part of *pilau* is the crispy layer of browned rice on top, made by baking the finished dish in the oven. *Mchicha*, a variety of spinach grown locally all over East Africa, is often cooked with coconut as an everyday dish.

Ingredients

4 cups basmati rice

6 cups water

500 g fish, cut into cubes

2 cloves of garlic, minced

1 2-cm piece of ginger, minced

1 teaspoon each cinnamon, coriander seeds and cumin seeds

1/2 teaspoon cardamom

1/4 cup vegetable oil

4 teaspoons tomato paste

250 g boiled potatoes, halved

2 onions, chopped

for the coconut mchicha

500 g spinach, washed and coarsely chopped

250 g tomatoes, chopped

1 onion, chopped

2 tablespoons vegetable oil

1/2 cup coconut milk

Preheat the oven to 180°C. Heat the oil in a large saucepan and gently fry the fish on medium heat until cooked and slightly browned. Remove the fish with a slotted spoon and set aside. Add the onions, garlic and ginger to the pan and sauté until fragrant. Add the spices, the tomato paste and the rice and sauté for another few minutes until the rice has absorbed the spices and is becoming slightly clear. Add the water, fish and potato pieces. Cover and turn the heat to low. Simmer for 20 minutes, checking periodically to see if you need to add a bit more water. Remove from heat and put into an oven dish and cover with aluminium foil. Bake for another 20 minutes and serve hot.

To make the spinach, sauté the onions in the oil over medium heat. When they begin to turn golden, add the tomatoes and cook until they begin to break down. Add the spinach and stir regularly until it wilts. Add the coconut milk and simmer, uncovered, for another 10 minutes. Serve hot.

Swahili Pudini

Say the name of this traditional Swahili dessert fast enough and you will soon discover its origins – steeped in the colonial tradition of English steamed puddings. Despite its northern roots, *pudini* has become a central part of Swahili weddings and important occasions. As the groom meets his bride for the first time, a large dish of this baked custard is served for all the guests to enjoy.

Ingredients
100 g plus 1/2 cup sugar
2 litres milk
8 eggs
1/2 teaspoon cardamom pods
50 g raisins
2 tablespoons water

Preheat an oven to 180°C. In a heavy saucepan, bring the cardamom seeds and the milk to the boil. Remove from heat and leave it to infuse for 5 minutes. Meanwhile, whisk the eggs and 100 g of sugar together until thoroughly mixed. Pour the milk into the egg and sugar mixture.

In a small saucepan, boil the 1/2 cup of sugar and 2 tablespoons of water until the sugar dissolves, stirring frequently. When it turns a rich golden colour, remove from the heat and pour it into a 20-cm fixed-bottom mould. Add the milk, eggs and sugar, then the raisins. Make a water bath by filling a shallow pan with boiling water and setting the mould inside. Gently bake for 45 minutes or until the custard is set, checking periodically to make sure the water in the bath hasn't boiled away and topping it up as needed. Cool and refrigerate for 1 hour. Before serving, turn upside down onto a serving plate.

Kipungani Explorer

Located on the far side of Lamu Island, the waterfront bungalows of Kipungani Explorer are a beachcomber's paradise. The lodge's remote and secluded location gives it a castaway feel and all its structures are made from materials found around the island. Each of the private cottages was built with nature in mind – palm-thatched *makuti* roofs shelter straw-coloured walls of woven *mkeka* mats and bamboo blinds. When the sun descends in the evening, guests gather for sundowners at Kipungani's bar, built on stilts above the water to better enjoy the view of departing *dhow* fishing boats and storks roosting high in mangrove trees for the night.

Dining at Kipungani is an incredibly romantic experience. On clear nights, tables are set up under the stars to watch moonrise and guests settle back for some serious stargazing between courses of classic continental favourites and local Swahili specialities. In the main area, old maps of the Lamu Archipelago and the surrounding coast hang on the walls next to bowls of shells and suspended driftwood mobiles that twirl in the breeze. Large clam shells and long pieces of driftwood lean against the walls, adding to the castaway atmosphere. In the morning, full breakfasts can be served in the the shaded veranda of each room. Should guests prefer to dine on the beach, tables and chairs are set up on the sand for a private meal just above the lapping waves.

Kipungani's chefs pride themselves on knowing and catering to each guests' special favourites. Their cooking incorporates local ingredients in fresh and innovative ways, like pumpkin leaf or banana coconut soup, always served with fresh bread and plenty of vegetables. Swahili specialities like seafood *mchuzi* and *biriyani* are regularly presented beside classic favourites like crepes suzette, dark chocolate mousse and lemon tarts. Hot tea and plates of spice cake are brought to each banda in the late afternoon, once guests have worked up an appetite from beach combing, swimming or just walking the shores. At Kipungani, meals become a personal and intimate experience, served with all the panache and style of continental dining infused with the flavours of the Swahili Coast.

Prawns with Coconut Chutney
Banana Coconut Soup
Chicken Biriyani
Spiced Rice Cake

Prawns with Coconut Chutney

Indian cooking, with its use of coconut and spices, has played a special part in Swahili cuisine. No dish of Indian origin would be complete without a small dish of chutney or pickles served alongside. Although both can can be made from any variety of fresh ingredients, mango, carrot and coconut chutneys are the most popular.

Ingredients

16 jumbo prawns, cleaned and peeled but with tails intact

2 tablespoons lime juice

1 tablespoon white wine

4 cloves of garlic, crushed

a pinch each of salt and pepper

90 g desiccated coconut

3 tablespoons fresh coriander, finely chopped

2 tablespoons flour

2 eggs, lightly beaten

vegetable oil for frying

2 limes, deseeded and cut into wedges

for the chutney

1 cup grated or desiccated coconut

juice of 4 lemons or limes

1/2 teaspoon salt

2 tablespoons water

1 tablespoon vegetable oil

To make the chutney, blend all the ingredients together well and chill until ready to serve.

Combine the juice, white wine, garlic, salt and pepper in a medium bowl and add the prawns. Stir to coat, cover and refrigerate in the marinade for at least 1 hour. Drain the prawns and pat dry. In a small bowl, mix the coconut and coriander and set aside. Pour the flour into a plastic bag and add the prawns, shaking to coat well. Remove the prawns, shake off the extra flour and dip them in the beaten eggs and then directly into the bowl of coconut and fresh coriander. Heat about two fingers of oil in a large frying pan until it splutters when you add a few drops of water. Using a slotted spoon, carefully add the prawns, a few at a time, and deep fry until brown and crispy on both sides. Remove and serve with chutney and the lime wedges.

Banana Coconut Soup

Plantains are a staple of people's diet throughout sub-Saharan Africa, and the Swahili Coast is no exception. All over villages and *shamba* farms, clusters of banana trees grow in thick clumps and women sell the fruit straight from the stalk along roadsides and at the market. During the monsoon rains, banana leaves are big enough to be cut straight from the tree and used as makeshift umbrellas.

Ingredients

4 medium plantain bananas
2 tablespoons olive oil
1 medium onion, chopped
1 clove of garlic, crushed
2 cups chicken stock
1 cup coconut milk
freshly chopped coriander, to garnish

Preheat the oven to 180°C. Place the whole plantains, unpeeled, on a tray and bake for about 30 minutes, or until soft. When they have cooled, peel the plantains and cut the fruit into pieces. Heat the oil in a medium saucepan and fry the onions and garlic until soft and only beginning to colour. Pour in the stock and coconut milk and bring to a boil. Cover and simmer gently for 5 minutes. Remove from the heat, add the plantain pieces

and puree in a blender until smooth. Return to the pan and simmer until heated through. Serve hot garnished with fresh coriander.

Chicken Biriyani

Biriyani is a traditional festival dish along the East African coast, a special meal made during religious feasts, when marriages are celebrated or important company comes to dinner. Although its basic elements – spicy rice served with a meat or fish based *mchuzi* stew – are the same, recipes for *biriyani* vary from family to family and are often closely guarded secrets. Here, the chefs at Kipungani share theirs. Serve with *chapati* or pilau.

Ingredients

1 whole chicken cut into 8 pieces, or 8 assorted chicken pieces
2 onions, chopped

1 tablespoon fresh ginger, finely chopped

2 cloves of garlic, crushed

1 teaspoon each of cloves, cardamom seeds, black peppercorns, cumin seeds, powdered coriander, powdered cumin, turmeric and chilli powder

1 medium-sized cinnamon stick

1 cup tomatoes, chopped

1 cup plain yoghurt

2 tablespoons fresh coriander, chopped, plus more for garnish

salt to season

2 tablespoons butter

225 g potatoes, boiled, peeled, and cut into pieces

a handful of fresh coriander, chopped, to garnish

In a large saucepan, melt the butter over medium heat. Add the onion and the cloves, cardamom, black peppercorns, cumin seeds and cinnamon stick and stir until the onion is soft and beginning to brown. Add the garlic and ginger, and before the garlic begins to colour add the powdered spices – the coriander, cumin, turmeric and chilli powder. Stir to mix well. Add the chopped tomatoes and the fresh coriander. Stir when cooking so that the sauce doesn't stick to the bottom of the pan. When the tomato has reduced, add the yoghurt and the chicken, stirring to coat. Cover and let simmer for about 20 minutes, or until the chicken is well cooked. About 10 minutes before it's ready, add the boiled potatoes. Serve hot garnished with fresh coriander.

Spiced Rice Cake

Swahili cakes are usually baked with coconut milk and scented with sweet spices like cardamom and cinnamon. Perfect for those with wheat intolerance, this cake is delicious on its own but is great served with custard sauce. For a traditional end to your Swahili meal, serve it with ginger tea or *kahawa*.

Ingredients

250 g butter

1 cup sugar

2 eggs, separated

1 teaspoon vanilla

300 g rice flour

seeds from 3 cardamom pods, lightly crushed with the back of a knife

1 teaspoon ground cinnamon

1/4 cup coconut milk

Preheat the oven to 180°C. Cream together the butter, sugar and vanilla until light and fluffy. Add the egg yolks and beat well. In another bowl, sift together the rice flour and the spices. Add a little of the dry mixture to the butter and sugar and then a little of the coconut milk, alternating until everything is mixed. In a separate bowl, beat the egg whites until they are stiff. Using a metal spoon, gently fold them into the cake batter. Spread into a greased 20-cm tin lined with baking parchment. Bake for about 30-35 minutes, or until a skewer comes out clean when inserted into the centre.

Munira's Camp

High on a sand ridge on remote Kiwayu Island, just sixty kilometres south of the Somali border, Munira's Camp is an exceptional property in an unsurpassed location. For sheer remoteness and untouched simplicity, there's nothing like it on the East African coast. Long deserted beaches stretch for miles, ridged with sand dunes spotted with scrub bush and acacia trees. Just offshore, acres of coral extend into Kiungu National Marine Reserve, a protected area that stretches all the way to Somalia.

The main area of Munira's Camp looks out towards the eastern side of Kiwayu, where the islands of the Lamu Archipelago meet the mainland's Dodori Game Reserve and Boni Forest Reserve. The view is beyond incredible – perched on the ridge of the island, the water is visible from either side. After a morning spent snorkelling around the plentiful reefs that border the island, lunch is served on the eastern beach in the shade a rustic *makuti* shelter, where a spacious hammock is perfect for watching the waves. There, a barbecue is set up, with tables in the shade facing the long stretch of deserted sand. Back at the main area, hand-blown glass buoys tied in coconut ropes hang from the rafters and mobiles made from coral and cuttlefish shells blow gently in the afternoon breeze.

Dinner is served on *makuti* mats around a communal table, but not before sunset – accompanied by ample sundowners and the infamous *dawa* cocktail of vodka, honey, and lime – is thoroughly enjoyed. A telescope is never far from the table and owner Mike Kennedy, a stargazer at heart, knows exactly where Jupiter will rise that night. A hanging bed and a low sitting area plied with *kikoi*-covered pillows create a sociable area for after-hours relaxation. Once the stars are out and the moon is shining, a four-course dinner is served under the bright African sky, the horizon shadowed in darkness, the lights of civilisation far from sight. During full moon, you don't even need your lantern – the sandy path back to your private beach banda is illuminated in an ethereal and almost heavenly glow.

Sunset Soup
Spicy Prawn Kebabs with Coconut Sauce
Swahili Crab served with Tamarind Potatoes
Date Cake

Sunset Soup

Sunset is a special time of day at Munira's Camp. The dry heat of the late afternoon begins to abate as the sun sinks closer and closer to the western side of Kiwayu, the mangrove islands and the endless expanses of the Dodori Game Reserve reaching far towards the horizon. Bit by bit, it descends from the sky, changing the landscape into far-flung oranges, yellows, and reds — much like the colour of this aptly named soup.

Ingredients

50 g pumpkin flesh

1 mango, peeled and deseeded

1 orange, peeled and deseeded

1 1/2 carrot, peeled

1 onion

2 medium tomatoes

1 medium potato, peeled

2 tablespoons butter

500 ml vegetable or chicken stock

Chop all of the ingredients together and in a medium saucepan, melt the butter and fry the onion over medium heat until soft. Add the tomato and pumpkin, and continue to sauté for about 4 minutes. Add the mango, orange, carrot and potato, and sauté for another 2 minutes. Pour in the stock and if the soup is too thick, add some extra hot water. Simmer over low heat for about 15 minutes or until the vegetables and fruit are tender. Puree in a blender, return to the heat, season to taste and serve.

Spicy Prawn Kebabs with Coconut Sauce

The cooking at Munira's is fresh and natural, the flavours a perfect blend of rich spices and fresh ingredients. Here, prawns marinated in Arabian spices are grilled over an open fire — perfect food when you've just returned from a snorkelling trip around the island. Although the kebabs are delicious when served with coconut sauce, they are just as good on their own.

Ingredients

500 g king-sized prawns, cleaned

3 limes, juiced

1 clove of garlic, crushed

1/2 teaspoon each cumin, coriander and chilli powder

1/2 teaspoon turmeric

1 tablespoon olive oil

salt and pepper to taste

4 bamboo skewers, soaked in water for 20 minutes

for the coconut sauce

1/2 cup coconut milk

2 tablespoons vegetable oil

4 medium tomatoes, peeled and chopped

1 small onion, chopped

1 teaspoon turmeric

1 teaspoon curry powder

1/2 stock cube

salt and pepper to taste

Mix all of the ingredients for the prawns together in a shallow bowl and marinate in the refrigerator for at least 30 minutes, but longer if possible. Meanwhile, make the coconut sauce. Heat the oil in a medium frying pan and sauté the onion until soft. Add the tomatoes and cook for about 4 minutes or until they are starting to soften. Add the spices, the stock cube, and the coconut milk. Simmer for another 3 minutes, season to taste and set aside.

When the prawns have finished marinating, slide them onto the bamboo skewers and grill on the barbecue for about 3 minutes on each side or until their flesh is opaque and beginning to turn pink. Served topped with the coconut sauce.

Swahili Crab served with Tamarind Potatoes

Crabs love mangrove forests and although Kiwayu Island's beach is a 14-km stretch of deserted white sand, on the western side of the island mangrove inlets and narrow waterways made the perfect place for crabs to thrive. What better way to take advantage of the bounty of the ocean than to serve them baked with a smattering of ginger, lime, chilli and white wine?

Ingredients

4 crabs, boiled with their meat removed (but keep the shell)

1/2 onion, minced

2 tablespoons olive oil

3 cloves of garlic, chopped

2-cm of fresh ginger, chopped

1 teaspoon chilli powder

15 ml gin

15 ml white wine

15 ml white vinegar

2 limes, juiced

1 teaspoon each fresh parsley and rosemary

1 tablespoon flour

1 tablespoon butter

50 g gouda cheese

1/2 cup milk

for the tamarind potatoes

500 g potatoes, peeled and halved

3 tomatoes, finely chopped

1 onion, finely chopped

3 cloves of garlic, finely chopped

1 teaspoon each powdered coriander and cumin

1 teaspoon curry powder

1 teaspoon turmeric

1 teaspoon chilli powder

50 g tamarind pulp

4 tablespoons vegetable oil

In a large saucepan, gently fry the onion in the olive oil until soft. Add 2 cloves of garlic, the chilli powder and ginger and continue to sauté for about 2 minutes over low heat. Add the chopped crab meat and sauté for another 2 minutes. Evenly divide the mixture among the reserved crab shells.

In another saucepan, melt the butter and add the flour, stirring evenly to let in cook for a few seconds. Pour in the milk and stir to prevent lumps from forming. Add the gin, white wine, white vinegar, lime juice, herbs and cheese and cook over medium heat, stirring constantly, until the sauce thickens. Pour the white wine sauce over the crabs and serve.

To make the potatoes, fry the onion in vegetable oil in a large saucepan until soft. Add the tomatoes and garlic, and cook for 3 minutes. Add the potatoes and spices, and stir to combine. Pour 3 cups of hot water over the mixture, cover and boil for 20 minutes. In the meantime, pour about 3 tablespoons of boiling water over the tamarind pulp and set aside. When the potatoes are tender, strain the tamarind liquid and add it to the saucepan, seasoning with salt and pepper to taste.

Date Cake

Dates are a speciality of the Arab world, where dry desert sands hold little sustenance for weary travellers. In this delectable dessert, dates are used to make a sweet moist cake rich with deep flavours. I suggest doubling the quantity of the caramel you make because as soon as you try some it will be impossible not to eat it from the bowl with a spoon.

Ingredients
250 g butter
125 g flour
2 teaspoons baking powder
5 eggs
125 g sugar
1/4 cup milk
250 g dried dates and 1/2 cup hot water
1 teaspoon instant coffee or 15 ml strong coffee
for the caramel
2 tablespoons butter
3 tablespoons sugar
1/2 tin condensed milk or cream
1 vanilla pod

Preheat the oven to 180°C. In a large bowl, cream the butter and sugar together. Add the eggs and beat until smooth. Add the flour and baking powder, then the milk, stirring gently until mixed. Butter and flour a 20-cm by 30-cm and pour the batter in, baking for about 40 minutes. Let cool before adding the caramel topping.

To make the caramel, melt the butter over very low heat and add the sugar, stirring continuously until melted. Add the condensed milk and the vanilla pod and continue to stir for about 2 more minutes. Remove from the heat, remove the vanilla pod and allow the caramel to cool completely before pouring it over the top of the cake. Chill before serving.

SWAHILI WAY
Halua

Served as a treat during auspicious occasions and Islamic holidays, *halua* has a special place in the culinary life of the Swahili Coast. Because *halua* is made through a labour-intensive process that requires several hours of constant stirring and intense supervision, it is only cooked in special shops where carefully guarded recipes are handed down from one generation to the next. A well-stoked fire slowly heats a large copper pan which is firmly anchored to the floor. The *halua* maker pours varying proportions of sugar and water into the pan and begins to stir the heated mixture by hand, a process that last for several hours. He constantly sifts and stirs what will eventually become a viscous syrup, removing its impurities and letting it slowly thicken. Although *halua* can be made of differing ingredients and flavourings, the most popular flavour is a plain sugar base delicately scented with rose water.

Mombasa

*Bahari haivukwi kwa
kuogelea.
An ocean is not crossed
by swimming.*

Serena Beach Hotel

It's rare to find food at a large hotel as original and innovative as dining at the Serena Beach Hotel, where classic Swahili tastes mix with contemporary favourites to create a versatile menu of wholesome, fresh cooking. Meals at the Serena are intimate affairs where the garden and ocean are never out of sight. From romantic sundowners on the rooftop terrace as a Swahili pianist plays light jazz to meals taken in the central courtyard bordered by a long ornamental pool and the classic exterior of the main stone building, each of the dining areas authentically evokes the traditions of the Swahili Coast.

Along the palm-fringed beaches of Mombasa's north coast, the Jahazi Grill stands out as an example of classic seafood dining seeped in Swahili style. From the waterfront, its exterior looks like the prow of a traditional *jahazi*, the largest of the Indian Ocean sailing boats, its entrance rising towards the waterfront as if it is about to set sail on the white-capped waves. Inside, fine sand covers the floor to add an authentic beach front feel to interior dining. Sails of cream coloured *marekani* cloth drape from the high ceiling and flutter in the ocean breeze. Slatted wooden shutters open to gardens, palm trees and the beach front just outside. Each table is covered with a colourful *kanga* cloth, the bright shades of the geometric designs complementing the calm neutrals of the whitewashed walls, dark shutters and pale sand.

Large stretches of frangipani trees and towering coconut palms make the Serena Beach Hotel's gardens an elegant feature of the Mombasa property, and each of the hotel's restaurants uses the surrounding verdure to add a touch of tropical elegance to hotel dining. The courtyard of the main dining room is shaded with large flowering vines that open their purple and white flowers to the morning sun. A small fountain trickles nearby, bringing the peaceful sound of water to the classic Swahili interior. Traditional kitchen implements like the *mbuzi* coconut grater and *uteo* winnowing baskets line the walls, evoking the timeless cooking and local flavours of the Swahili Coast.

Palm Heart Salad
Spicy Coconut Soup
Lobster Fricassee
Plantain Banana

Palm Heart Salad

Mombasa, with its profusion of palm trees, that is perfect place to find *kitale*, the vegetable 'heart' of the palm tree and is popularly called the 'rich man's salad.' A whole *kitale*, or palm heart, is about 50cm long and when peeled and boiled, gives this gentle salad a rich lemon colour.

Ingredients
500 g palm heart stalk
juice of 2 lemons
2 tablespoons olive oil

Remove the outer husks from the palm heart, clean well to remove all the dirt and slice into quarters lengthways. Thinly slice each quarter and place all the kitale in a salad bowl. Add the lemon juice and olive oil and toss well, making sure that all of the slices are well coated with dressing. Season to taste and serve.

Spicy Coconut Soup

In the west, coconuts are usually used in sweet cooking – as an ingredient for macaroons, pies or cakes. On the Swahili Coast, coconut milk is used as a base for everything from *mchuzi* stew to doughy yeast breads. This soup uses spices to evoke the coconut's savoury flavour and is hearty and instantly soothing.

Ingredients
60 g butter
1 large onion, chopped
30 g curry powder
250 ml chicken stock
250 ml coconut milk
1 green papaya, peeled and deseeded
120 g grated coconut
250 ml double cream
In a large saucepan, heat the butter over low heat. Add the onions and cook slowly until they become

translucent, but don't let them colour. Add the curry powder and fry gently for about 3 minutes, stirring constantly. Pour in the stock and coconut milk, then add the papaya. Simmer for another 5 minutes or until the papaya is tender. Place the soup in a blender along with the grated coconut and the cream and puree until smooth. Season to taste and serve hot or cold.

Lobster Fricassee

This fricassee is something of an *mchuzi* dish, where seafood, fish, vegetables or meat are cooked with a blend of spices and coconut milk to create a rich and hearty stew. Although lobster is not traditionally used as a main element in *mchuzi*, the rich blend of spices and coconut here draws out its gentle flavour.

Ingredients

4 lobsters, about 750g each

200 g unsalted butter
1 onion
4 cloves of garlic
1/4 teaspoon cardamom powder
1/2 teaspoon cinnamon powder
600 ml fish stock
600 ml coconut milk
pinch of cayenne pepper
pinch of black pepper
optional cream or yoghurt, to thicken

Remove the lobster meat from its shell and cut into medallions. In a large pan, melt the butter and sauté the onions and garlic for about 2 minutes, or until fragrant but not coloured. Turn up the heat and add the lobster medallions, tossing to coat them with the butter, onions, and garlic. After a few minutes, add the cinnamon,

cardamom, black pepper and salt to taste. Stir again to coat the lobster well. If the mixture looks like it is starting to colour or burn, turn down the heat. After everything is well coated, add the fish stock and coconut milk. Simmer for another 2 minutes and if you like, add a few tablespoons of cream of yoghurt to thicken. Serve with coconut rice.

Plantain Banana

Plantains are a large variety of banana whose texture stands up to long cooking. It's delicate flavours are only slightly sweet and in this recipe the coconut milk, sugar, and cardamom lightly complement its delicate flavour. This dish can be served hot or cold and is especially nice with some golden sultanas scattered over the top.

Ingredients
4 plantain bananas
1 cup grated coconut
500 ml coconut milk
3 tablespoons sugar
1 teaspoon cardamom powder

Gently toast or fry the grated coconut until it begins to colour slightly and set it aside for later. With the skin still on, wash each plantain thoroughly. Cut them lengthways, then into quarters and remove the pith in the centre. Place all the pieces in a large saucepan. Pour coconut milk over the plantains and make sure they are covered – add more coconut milk if necessary. Over medium heat, bring the mixture to the boil and add the sugar and cardamom. Simmer until the coconut milk has reduced to a thick sauce and the plantains are soft but still firm. Add the toasted coconut, simmer a few minutes more, and remove from the heat. Serve hot or cold.

Alfajiri Villas

Alfajiri blends Swahili influences with all the passion of an Italian kitchen, and eating is a serious affair. Meals at the villas combine the best of both regional kitchens to produce authentic and original flavours – bowls of pasta steaming with olive oil and local vegetables, spiced *mchuzi* dishes of fish and seafood salsa and a procession of desserts that include home-made hazelnut ice cream and a medley of coconut-inspired treats. Local spices, all freshly ground and blended to perfection, flavour the dishes that make up each carefully selected menu and meals are made to order, tailored to the guests' individual tastes and personal favourites.

The villas' dining room is an open space where waves breaking on the beach below carry easily on the night air. Just metres away, the infinity pool shimmers and glows in the evening light, *kikoi*-inspired towels placed in a giant clam shell at its edge for a tempting after-dinner swim. At the bottom of the garden, a small wooden door unlatches to the beach, the waves at high tide reaching all the way to the sloping steps. Frangipani, succulent aloe and desert rose grow rampant in the sculpted gardens, releasing their scent into the thick night air.

An elaborate table, hand-carved by local craftsmen, stands in the centre of the dining room, its edges fringed in a geometric pattern that is a motif throughout the villas. Clay busts by a local Kikiyu artist, each sculpted portrait a profile of the tribes of Kenya, stand sentinel, the exquisite faces of Masai warriors and Samburu women looking out towards the tumultuous ocean. A large Iranian urn, hand-picked from the old town in Mombasa, forms the centrepiece of the dining room table, it's deep contours filled with sweet-scented frangipani flowers and fuchsia bougainvillaea. A West African *kuba* textile, its rough surface embroidered with beads and cowrie shells, runs the length of the table, but the most impressive feature is without doubt the Moroccan chandelier. Made of thin goatskin hand-painted with henna, six small lampshades hang gently above the table, effusing a magical light reminiscent of fireflies and enchantment, African style.

Seafood Salad with Red Pepper Dressing
Spaghetti ya Mboga
Prawn and Calamari Masala
Coconut Pie

Seafood Salad with Red Pepper Dressing

Seafood salad is a popular Italian starter and the perfect opening to a light meal served in the sun. The salad – a simple affair of boiled vegetables and seafood spiced with basil and olive oil – is complemented by the vibrant colour of the red pepper dressing, which adds a sweet tang to its classic Italian flavours.

Ingredients
80 g calamari, thinly sliced
80 g octopus, cut into small chunks
12 medium prawns, cleaned and peeled
1 zucchini, cut into thin strips
1 carrot, cut into thin strips
2 stalks celery, cut into thin strips
1/2 white onion, cut into thin strips
a handful of basil, cut into thin strips
4 tablespoons olive oil
1 litre vegetable stock
salt and black pepper
for the dressing
300 g red pepper, cut into chunks
100 g white onions, cut into chunks
4 tablespoons vinegar
4 tablespoons olive oil
2 tablespoons white sugar
1 teaspoon salt
1/4 cup cream

In a large saucepan, bring the stock to the boil and blanch the vegetables for a few minutes. Drain, but keep the stock and bring it back to the boil. Add the seafood and cook until soft. Drain again and set the seafood and vegetables aside. In a small bowl mix the basil, olive oil, salt and black pepper. In your serving bowl, toss the seafood and vegetables together with the dressing until well coated, and serve.

To make the dressing, mix the ingredients together in a small saucepan and cook for about 20 minutes over low heat. Add a little water if the mixture starts to stick. Remove from the heat and puree in a blender. Strain and mix with fresh cream before serving over the seafood salad.

Spaghetti ya Mboga

Pasta is a perennial favourite at Alfajiri, and aside from the traditional Italian sauces the chef has created a blend of local vegetables, spices and Italian elements that makes a hearty treat after a day spent beach combing and wading through tide pools. *Ya mboga* means 'with vegetables' in Swahili.

Ingredients

1 zucchini, cut into cubes

1 aubergine, cut into cubes

vegetable oil, for frying

1 onion, finely chopped

1/2 red bell pepper, thinly sliced

1/2 yellow bell pepper, thinly sliced

a handful of coriander, coarsely chopped

1 hot chilli, minced

1 clove of garlic, minced

1 tablespoon capers

12 green olives, deseeded and sliced

6 tablespoons olive oil

1 cup tomato paste

6 tomatoes, cubed

450 g spaghetti

In a deep pan, fry the zucchini and aubergine cubes until they are coloured and soft. Drain and set aside.

Bring a large pot of water to the boil, add a generous amount of salt and let it simmer, covered.

In a large non-stick pan, cook the onion in olive oil until golden brown. Add the garlic, chillies, vegetables and coriander. Cover and cook for 5 minutes, then add the capers, olives and tomato paste and cook for another 5 minutes, still covered. As the sauce is cooking, add the spaghetti to the boiling water and cook until al dente, for about 7 minutes. Season the sauce, drain the pasta and toss together well before serving.

Prawn and Calamari Masala

Swahili food has strong Indian elements, and this particular dish brings out the best in both cooking traditions. A *masala* is a special blend of spices, the proportions of which are usually a carefully guarded secret – but the chef at Alfajiri is generous enough to share. Feel free to increase the amount of spices at your discretion. This *masala* is best when served with *pilau* or *chapati*.

Ingredients

320 g calamari, thinly sliced

12 medium prawns, cleaned and peeled

2 cloves of garlic, minced

1 medium onion, minced

a finger-sized piece of fresh ginger, peeled and minced

a handful of fresh coriander, chopped

1 hot chilli, thinly sliced

1 teaspoon cumin seeds

1/2 teaspoon powdered coriander

1/2 teaspoon powdered cumin

2 teaspoons garam masala

1/2 teaspoon turmeric powder

1/4 teaspoon curry powder

2 cups tomatoes, peeled and finely chopped

6 tablespoons vegetable oil

Heat the vegetable oil in a large non-stick pan and cook the onions until browned. Add the garlic, spices and seafood and stir-fry the mixture until the calamari is opaque in colour. Add the tomatoes and chillies and simmer until the sauce is thick – about 10 minutes. Season to taste and garnish with fresh coriander.

Coconut Pie

Coconut is a staple ingredient of cooking all over the Swahili Coast, but is usually used in savoury dishes like *mchuzi* or rice. In this recipe, coconut forms the base of a sweet pie or tart – a soft and comforting dessert . To add another Swahili element to your meal, serve coconut pie with ginger tea.

Ingredients
for the pastry shell
125 g icing sugar
250 g flour
125 g butter
2 eggs for the filling
200 g grated coconut
200 g sugar
12 egg yolks
750 ml milk
300 ml cream

Preheat the oven to 180°C. Mix all the ingredients for the pastry in a bowl until the mixture comes together in a soft ball. On a piece of waxed paper, roll the dough out and flip it into a pie dish. Prick the bottom with a fork and bake the pastry shell blind until brown – about 30 minutes. Remove from the oven, but leave the oven on. Meanwhile, make the filling. Mix all the filling ingredients until well blended. Pour everything into the baked pastry shell and return to the oven for another 40 minutes, or until the filling has set. Remove and serve cold.

Funzi Keys

Dining at Funzi Keys is always a personal experience. For starters, there's no menu – each guest decides what they want to eat for each meal on a daily basis and the choice is truly staggering. Chefs at Funzi cook from a dazzling array of culinary traditions, from traditional Swahili and comforting Italian to ethnic Indian and Chinese. So versatile is the kitchen that it's impossible not to feel spoiled. From king-sized grilled prawns served with spicy potatoes to bowls of crab curry and coconut rice, Funzi Keys makes sure you get exactly what you want, cooked the way you want, all of the time.

Guests at Funzi decide where they want to eat as well, and there are plenty of options to choose from. The spacious dining room centres around a mangrove tree that lights up at night, as if a web of fireflies have been caught in an invisible net. At its base, traditional Swahili coffee pots and large bowls create a glow of copper colours that shimmer and shine in the light of hurricane lanterns. From each upstairs table, a small reflection pool and a wide open view add irresistible romance. A thousand stars are visible and the moon is reflected over the water, the outline of patchwork islands dark against the night sky.

Meals are a creative experience at Funzi Keys. Romantic dinners can be had in the seclusion of a private bonfire on the beach beside each of the rooms, the high tide lapping gently against the deserted shore. Personal dining is an inexorable part of the Funzi experience. A large *jahazi* sailing boat is anchored just off the island and each evening guests can embark on a sunset cruise around the keys, sailing through still waters and sometimes spying dolphins along the way. Lunch is often taken by the pool side, where the sparkling blue water blends easily with the Indian Ocean just metres away. Dinner on the beach is a highlight of every stay, with an opulent setting of low tables and ample cushions surrounded by suspended lanterns, the waves lapping lazily against the seashell-strewn sand.

Cold Avocado Soup
Calamari with Peri Peri Sauce
Swahili Lobster with Coconut Rice
Passion Fruit Mousse

Cold Avocado Soup

Chilled soups make a great starter during hot summer days and this pale green soup is as refreshing as it is attractive. Press your finger into the avocado to tell if it's ripe – it should yield easily to pressure.

Ingredients
1 ripe avocado
250 ml milk
500 ml chicken stock, cold
2 red onions, chopped
2 tablespoons vegetable oil
salt and pepper

Halve the avocado, remove the seed, and scoop out the fruit with a spoon. Blend with the chopped onion in a food processor and add the stock and milk until everything is well mixed. Season to taste and serve chilled.

Calamari with Peri Peri Sauce

Calamari cooks quickly and is one of the easiest types of seafood to prepare. Here, it's given a Mediterranean flavour with plenty of lemon, parsley, garlic and white wine.

Ingredients
800 g calamari, cleaned
1 leek, sliced finely
1 onion, chopped
3 cloves of garlic, minced
1 handful fresh parsley, minced
juice of 1 lemon
1 shot brandy
1/2 glass white wine
salt and pepper
vegetable oil, for frying

Slice the calamari into small squares and with a sharp knife cut a criss-cross pattern into one side. In a medium frying pan sauté the leek, onion, garlic and calamari for about 3 minutes, stirring well. Season and while still in the pan add the lemon juice, brandy and white wine. Remove from heat and stir in the parsley. Serve hot.

Swahili Lobster with Coconut Rice

Coconut rice is an absolute classic in Swahili cooking. A mainstay of the traditional diet – and a delicious one at that – it can be found on tables from fishing villages to the most elegant hotels. Here, lobster cooked in coriander and coconut makes a soothing yet spicy main dish.

Ingredients
4 lobsters, 600g each
1 carrot, cubed
1 green pepper, cubed
1 handful fresh coriander, chopped

250 ml coconut milk
1 chicken stock cube
1 shot brandy
1 onion, chopped
2 cloves of garlic, chopped
500 g tomatoes, peeled and chopped
salt and pepper
for the coconut rice
2 cups basmati rice
2 cups water
250 ml coconut milk
salt

To make the lobster, halve it lengthways, rinse the shell and spoon out the meat. Cut it into cubes. (At this point, you can boil the shells to clean them and set them aside to use as a serving dish, if you like.) Sauté half of the chopped onion and all the carrot and sweet pepper. Remove from heat, season and set aside. In another pan, sauté the rest of the onion. When it begins to turn

translucent, add the lobster and sauté for 1 minute. Add the brandy – this will flambé it – and mix in the vegetables. Serve spooned into the lobster shell.

To make the coconut rice, bring the coconut milk and water to the boil in a large saucepan. Add a pinch of salt and the rice and cook covered over low heat until the rice is done – about 10-15 minutes. Add more water periodically if it looks like the liquid has run out. Serve hot.

Passion Fruit Mousse

Passion fruit grows in abundance all over the African tropics and is a delicious and refreshing treat. Here, a light mouse is made from the fruit pulp.

Ingredients
5 passion fruit

3 egg whites
75 g sugar
50 g corn flour
100 ml water
1 tablespoon gelatine powder

Halve the passion fruit – preserving the empty shells – and push the fruit pulp through a sieve to extract the juice. Mix in the water. In a medium saucepan, bring the juice to the boil and add the corn flour, stirring to thicken. Remove from the heat and cool.

Whip the egg whites until they form stiff peaks and mix in the sugar with a wooden spoon. Fold in the juice mixture and gelatine. Carefully – so as not to remove the air from the egg whites – spoon into the halves of the passion fruit and chill for at least 3 hours before serving.

Tamarind Dhow

Dining on the Tamarind Dhow is indubitably one of the classic experiences to be had on the Kenyan Coast. Setting sail twice a day from its private jetty in the old city's harbour, the large *jahazi* boat makes an impressive sight against the backdrop of Mombasa's waterfront and stone town. Once on board, guests are greeted with a classic *dawa* cocktail – a heady mix of honey, freshly squeezed limes and chilled vodka. Tables border the perimeter of the boat and afford easy views of Tudor Creek, Mombasa's old city and the wide expanses of the Indian Ocean.

As the wooden sailing boat sets off across calm waters, a local band plays soft music and a romantic atmosphere is cast. Sunset is a magical experience, set against the outlines of Fort Jesus and the Swahili buildings of old Mombasa town. After a pleasant sail through Tudor Creek, as the lights of the waterfront beckon invitingly across the water, the Tamarind's chefs set up their charcoal grills right on deck and before long the heady aromas of grilled lobster and Kenyan steak waft temptingly into the night air. After a four-course meal of fresh salads, spiced rice and Swahili grilled lobster, prawns and seafood, *kahawa* made of the finest highland Kenyan coffee is served the traditional way, steaming from shining copper pots into small china cups. As the smell of spiced coffee awakens senses pleasantly sated after a delectable meal, the night is only just beginning.

The Tamarind experience is more than just fine dining in stunning surroundings. After dinner is served the *jahazi* floats lazily in a quiet bay cloaked by high hills covered by mangrove and palm. A breeze rises off the Indian Ocean as the band plays Kenyan favourites and modern rhythms, the music lingering on deck before dissipating deep into the darkness. Guests dance the night away under the African sky, the stars and other diners their only companions. Late into the evening, the Tamarind Dhow often unfurls its white sails and as the wind swells, the boat tacks gently back and forth on its way back to harbour.

Dawa Coctail
Crab and Sweet Corn Soup
Samaki wa Kupaka
Coupe Bahari

Dawa Coctail

Cocktails are an enjoyable part of life in the tropics. Here, thick honey and freshly-squeezed lime create a delectable refreshment.

Ingredients
4 tablespoons honey
2 limes
1 shot vodka
crushed ice

Wash the skins of the limes to remove any waxy residue, slice them in half and remove the seeds. Juice the limes directly into your serving glass and add the squeezed limes to the bottom. Pour the honey over the juice and limes and add the vodka, stirring to mix well. Fill the rest of the glass with crushed ice and serve.

Crab and Sweet Corn Soup

The crab in this reciepe takes some preparation if you want to use fresh meat. If you buy your crab live, the most humane way of killing it is to place it in the freezer for an hour. Boil the crab in its shell for 15 minutes, then crack it open and remove the meat from its body and claws.

Ingredients
50 g crabmeat
60 ml sake
1 teaspoon salt
500 g fresh sweet corn off the cob
500 ml chicken stock
500 ml fish stock
a handful of fresh parsley, chopped for garnish
Simmer the corn and and stock in a large saucepan for

15 minutes. Puree in a blender and return to the heat for a few minutes. Just before serving, add the salt, crabmeat and sake. Serve hot and garnished with parsley.

Samaki wa Kupaka

Spicy and light, this grilled fish makes great barbecue food. Usually cooked over a traditional *jiko*, its blend of fresh coriander and ground spices smells as good as it tastes.

Ingredients
1 kg fish fillets (250 g each)
800 ml coconut cream
4 cloves of garlic, minced
1 2-cm piece fresh ginger, minced
2 teaspoons cayenne pepper
a handful of fresh coriander, chopped
50 g tamarind pulp to make 150 ml of liquid
2 teaspoons turmeric
1 teaspoon salt
juice of one lime

Season each of the fish fillets with the salt and lime juice. In a separate bowl, mix the garlic, ginger, coriander, turmeric, tamarind and 100 ml of the coconut cream to form a thick paste. Coat the fish fillets with the paste, then cover and refrigerate for at least 1 hour. Right before you cook the fish, warm the remaining coconut cream in a medium saucepan and add any of the leftover paste from the marinade. Heat a grill pan and cook the fish fillets on each side for 2 minutes – they should only sear and not be fully cooked. Gently slide the fillets into

the coconut cream and boil for a few minutes until fully cooked. Serve hot.

Coupe Bahari

Days get hot and humid in Mombasa and ice cream is always a welcome refreshment. Here, coconut ice cream is made into a splendid sundae with rum-soaked raisins and sliced bananas for a real tropical treat. Make sure you have all the ingredients assembled before you start to make the sundae.

Ingredients
4 generous scoops of coconut ice cream
40 g raisins
40 ml rum
4 bananas, sliced lengthways
100 ml sugar syrup
60 g white sugar

Chill or freeze your sundae glasses. Soak the raisins in the rum and sugar syrup for about 2 hours or until they are plump and swollen. Put the sugar in a small saucepan over medium heat and without stirring let it melt and bubble until it begins to caramelise, then set aside. This should talk about 3 or 4 minutes – don't let it burn. Add a spoonful of raisins to the bottom of each glass and stand the sliced bananas upright. Add the coconut ice cream, pour the caramelised sugar over the top and serve immediately.

The Moorings

Every town on the Swahili Coast has at least one place where expatriate residents and locals are greeted by name and the atmosphere is relaxed and sociable as the sun goes down. In Mombasa, it's Moorings, a waterfront restaurant set deep in the peaceful harbour of Mtwapa Creek. Owner Ute Sassoon is proud of her position as the creator of this lively weekend scene. Come sundown, the tables are crowded with regulars who chat and dine the night away with bottles of cold Tusker beer and plates of succulent fish and fresh seafood. On weekends, theme parties and fishing competitions keep the floating restaurant packed with people. During the day, boats dock and moor around the creek's peaceful waters, just a short distance from the open waters of the Indian Ocean.

The decor at Moorings is tasteful and simple, a subdued complement to the azure waters that surround it. Green palms and occasional baobab trees that rise up from the water's banks. A thatched *makuti* roof covers most of the pontoon, which rises at high tide. Wooden picnic tables are set up on the open deck for romantic evening dining and looking at the stars. Wicker and wood furniture is covered with blue *marekani* cloth to evoke the gentle waters just metres away. Water-skis and fishing trophies cover the walls and pillars, while traditional Swahili fishing traps serving as natural lampshades.

Moorings also runs a *dhow* cruise up and down the smooth waters of Mtwapa Creek. Lunchtime trips serve a tasty meal of seafood, fish and cold drinks, while sailing with sundowners is a particularly popular option for the evening crowd. As it cruises, the *dhow* passes palm groves and private houses, lavish gardens and forests of mangrove, the breeze off the ocean picking up as the *dhow* gets closer to open waters. Snacks of crispy fried prawns and fish, served with sweet honey and chilli sauce, appease the appetite on the journey. When the *dhow* reaches the mouth of Mtwapa Creek, the waterfront opens up to deeper waters as the Indian Ocean stretches distant against the wide horizon.

Crab Samosas
Deep-fried Honey Prawns
Honey Chicken and Pineapple
MishkakiTropical Fruit Salad

Crab Samosas

Samosas are a crispy deep-fried pastry that makes a popular daytime snack for people all over East Africa. Their small triangular shape, and the fact that they can be filled with any variety of meat, seafood, fish or vegetables means they're as versatile as they are delicious. If you don't want to make the *samosa* pastry yourself, many supermarkets now sell ready-made *samosa* dough.

Ingredients
for the filling
500 g crab meat
1 tablespoon butter
2 cloves of garlic, minced
1 teaspoon curry powder
1 teaspoon lemon juice
vegetable oil, for frying
for the samosa pastry
2 cups whole wheat flour
2/3 cup water

Make the dough first, since it will have to set for about 30 minutes. Mix the flour and water until it forms a firm but pliable dough – add more water or more flour if you need to. After kneading for a few minutes, roll it out to a thickness of about 1/8 cm. Place it gently on a floured baking sheet and allow it to rest in a warm, draught-free place (a cooled oven is great for this) and let it set.

Melt the butter over medium heat in a saucepan and add the garlic. When it's fragrant, add the crab meat, curry powder and lemon juice and season to taste. When the crab meat is opaque and well cooked, remove the filling from the heat and set aside.

Practice the following folding instructions with a piece of paper until you get the hang of it. It's not hard, and once you do one the rest will be easy. To make the traditional triangle-shape of a Swahili *samosa*, cut the rolled dough into a rectangle. Using a knife, make soft markings to divide the rectangle into two equal squares, a top square and a bottom square, and divide the top square into two triangles with a diagonal line extending from the top left to the bottom right. Now, place a generous spoonful of filling in the triangle on the left, being sure to leave enough room on the edges for the pastry to seal. Fold the right triangle over the left one so that their edges meet. Your dough should now be a left triangle over a bottom square. Now fold the entire bottom square right over the top triangle and wrap the last corner over the other side of the *samosa*.

Heat a generous amount of vegetable oil in a deep saucepan and deep-fry the *samosa* until they are golden brown on each side. Serve with a squeeze of lime.

Deep-fried Honey Prawns

Bitings are a perennial favourite at The Moorings and what better way to take advantage of the bounty of the ocean than serving hot snacks of deep-fried prawns, seeped in honey and coated with sesame seeds? Toasting the sesame seeds will require vigilance and low heat to make sure that they don't burn.

Ingredients
12 king-sized prawns, cleaned and peeled
4 tablespoons corn flour
vegetable oil, for frying
1/2 cup honey
1/4 cup sesame seeds, lightly toasted in a dry pan
for the batter
1/2 cup self-raising flour
1/2 cup corn flour
1 teaspoon lemon juice
3 tablespoons oil

Rinse the prawns in cold water and pat them dry with kitchen towels, then coat them with the corn flour and set aside. To make the batter, sift the flour and corn flour into a bowl and make a small well at the centre. In another bowl, mix the lemon juice and oil. Gradually add the liquid to the dry batter ingredients and beat well to make a smooth batter, adding more oil if the mixture is too thick.

Place the honey is a small saucepan and heat it gently over low heat. Set aside. In a deep frying pan, heat about two fingers of vegetable oil until it splutters when you add a few drops of water. Dip the corn flour prawns into the batter, coat well and using tongs or a slotted spoon, slip then into the hot oil. Fry, a few at a time, for about 2-3 minutes or until the prawns are crispy and golden brown on both sides. When they're done, remove them and place immediately into the warmed honey, tossing gently to coat. Place the prawns on a serving plate and sprinkle with toasted sesame seeds. Serve immediately.

Honey Chicken and Pineapple Mishkaki

Mishkaki are small pieces of meat or fish grilled over a *jiko* stove, and a popular Swahili snack at food stalls all over the coast. Here, The Moorings combines a traditional dish with contemporary flavours. The chicken pieces are marinated with a blend of honey and soy sauce and can be fried or grilled over the barbecue.

Ingredients
4 chicken breasts, deboned
1/4 cup soy sauce
1/2 cup honey
4 rounds of pineapple slices
8 bamboo skewers, soaked in water for 20 minutes
for the dipping sauce
2 tablespoons white vinegar
3 tablespoons honey
2 tablespoons soy sauce

Mix the soy sauce and honey in a deep bowl. Cut the chicken breasts into bite-sized cubes and marinate them in the soy sauce and honey mixture for at least 3 hours. Cut the pineapple into bite-sized triangles and place alternating pieces of pineapple and chicken on a bamboo skewer. Fry or grill the skewers until both the pineapple and the chicken are golden brown.

Mix the ingredients for the sauce in a small bowl and serve alongside the skewers.

Tropical Fruit Salad

With tropical fruits like pineapple, mangoes and passion fruit abundant on the East African coast, fruit salad makes a light and refreshing close to any meal. Here, the addition of Malibu lends a of touch of sophistication to this colourful fruit salad, made all the more delicious with a scoop of coconut ice cream.

Ingredients

1/2 pineapple, or 8 rounds
1 mango, deseeded and peeled
1/4 watermelon, deseeded
200 g green and purple grapes
1 tot Malibu coconut rum

Cut the pineapple, mango, and watermelon into bite-sized pieces. Cut the grapes in half and gently mix all the fruit together in a serving bowl. Sprinkle the Malibu over it and serve.

SWAHILI WAY
Kahawa

The drinking of *kahawa*, or spiced black coffee, has been a coastal tradition for centuries. Arab traders first brought coffee to the East African coast, where its preparation and traditions were soon adopted into Swahili culture. *Kahawa* is traditionally prepared in ornate brass braziers called *seredani*, where the coffee pot rests over a small bed of burning coals. The roasted beans are finely ground and mixed with water, cardamom seeds, ginger and sugar to taste. After simmering and almost coming to the boil, the *kahawa* is promptly poured into small porcelain cups and served immediately. Drinking coffee is a fundamental part of Swahili hospitality. When visitors arrive, tradition demands that *kahawa* be brewed, served and drunk before any serious business is discussed. It is this gesture of unerring hospitality – and the heady taste of spiced *kahawa* – that makes coffee drinking such an integral part of Swahili culture.

Zanzíbar

Safari ni hatua.
A long journey begins
with one step.

Zanzibar Serena Inn

Wander the narrow streets of Stone Town long enough and from the high stone houses and twisting passageways you'll come upon an open square where flamboyant trees gently drop their flame-coloured flowers and frangipani bend gently in the ocean breeze. Just beyond a row of tiled steps stand the open doors of the Zanzibar Serena Inn, where Swahili architecture and design takes on a cosmopolitan feel in the heart of the old city. Tiled fountains and tall white pillars create an atmosphere of elegant Swahili luxury, the Indian Ocean never far from sight. At the Zanzibar Serena Inn, colonial elements and Arabian style blend with a solid foundation of traditional Swahili decor to create an urban retreat in the heart of Stone Town as chic and sophisticated as it is unerringly traditional.

The head chefs at the Zanzibar Serena Inn mix Swahili traditions with international cuisine in an exciting take on fusion cooking. Spices are always included and used in creative ways, in everything from cinnamon bread to home-made ice cream in flavours like ginger, fresh vanilla and cardamom. Fish and seafood are selected personally each morning and afternoon at the Darajani Market on the edge of Stone Town, where fishermen from all over the west coast of the island bring their catch to auction. Continental favourites like prawn scampi and crab claws are given fresh new interpretations, served in a variety of sauces laced with coconut, cloves, ginger, coriander and lemon grass.

'Swahili Nights' at the Zanzibar Serena Inn is a popular weekly treat for visitors all over Stone Town. On the hotel's open terrace facing the sea, a barbecue of traditional Swahili specialities is set up in a beautiful display of colourful food, fresh tropical flowers and bright *kanga* cloths. A delectable buffet of traditional favourites like spinach in coconut cream, fish *mchuzi*, coconut rice, spiced seafood and savoury plantains is laid out for guests to sample and choose from. After dining, a live *taraab* band arrives to play the night away, the traditional Swahili music and drums resounding softly into the tropical night.

Fish Katlesi with Mango Pickle
Roast Tomato Soup
Nyama na Ndizi
Apple Rings in Vanilla Sauce

Fish Katlesi with Mango Pickle

Katlesi, or fried fish mixed with spices and potatoes, is a version of the Indian vegetarian speciality *bhaji*, a fried mixture of spices and mashed potatoes in batter. The batter for this mixture can be made ahead and fried just prior to serving. Mango pickle is another popular Indian addition to Swahili cuisine and this home-made version is well worth the effort for the colour and flavour it imparts to the hot *katlesi*.

Ingredients
160 g potatoes, mashed
2 onions, chopped
200 g fish fillet, cooked
salt and pepper
2 tablespoons vinegar

4 tablespoons flour
1 egg white
vegetable oil, to fry
for the mango pickle
1 unripe mango, peeled and sliced into julienne strips
2 teaspoons chilli powder
2 teaspoons turmeric powder
1 onion, sliced into julienne strips
1 carrot, sliced into julienne strips
1 green pepper, sliced into julienne strips
3 tablespoons vegetable oil
1 tablespoon tomato paste
2 tablespoons vinegar

Beat the potatoes, onion and fish fillet together until the mixture resembles a thick paste. Add the vinegar and

season to taste. Divide the mixture into 8 balls and form each one into a crescent shape. Heat a generous amount of vegetable oil in a deep frying pan until it splutters when you add a few drops of water. Dip each fish crescent first into the egg white, then the flour and place it gently into the oil. Fry, turning once, until the the fish is golden-brown and ready to serve.

To make the mango pickle, mix the mango with the chilli powder and turmeric and set aside. In a small saucepan, heat the vegetable oil and fry the onion, carrot and green pepper until slightly soft. Add the spiced mango, tomato paste and vinegar, then simmer until soft. Let cool before serving.

Roast Tomato Soup

In this recipe, Italian influences pervade a deeply flavoured soup that can be served either hot or cold, depending on the season. The oven-baked flavour of the roasted tomatoes and onions imparts a delicious depth to the soup and a handful of just-picked Italian herbs lends a light, fresh flavour.

Ingredients
500 g tomatoes
4 onions
3 tablespoons olive oil
a mixed handful of fresh rosemary, basil, oregano and thyme
500 ml vegetable stock
salt and pepper

Preheat the oven to 200°C. Place the tomatoes and 2 of the onions in a roasting tin and bake in the oven until soft and beginning to blacken. Remove and set aside. Sauté the remaining 2 onions in the olive oil and add the roasted tomatoes, onions and the stock. Simmer the mixture for 15 minutes, season, and puree before serving hot or cold.

Nyama na Ndizi

Mchuzi, or spiced stew, is a popular mainstay of the Swahili diet and can be enriched with anything from meat and seafood to seasonal vegetables. In this recipe, beef, or *nyama*, makes a hearty change from traditional island fare, and is served with savoury roasted bananas. Traditionally, the meat stew can also be served with coconut rice or *chapati*.

Ingredients

500 g beef, cubed

3 cloves of garlic, chopped

2-cm piece of fresh ginger, grated

2 teaspoons black pepper, ground

4 tablespoons vegetable oil

4 onions, sliced

5 tomatoes, diced

1 green pepper, diced

2 carrots, sliced

300 ml beef stock

4 plantains

Preheat the oven to 180°C. Peel the bananas, rub a little vegetable oil over them, and roast in a small tin for about 20 minutes or until they are soft and brown. Salt to taste. In a bowl, mix the beef, garlic, ginger and black pepper and marinate for at least 30 minutes, but preferably longer. Heat the oil in a large saucepan and add the beef, browning it well. Add the onions, green pepper and carrots and when they are beginning to soften, stir in the tomatoes. Once the tomatoes have reduced, stir in the beef stock. Serve beef *mchuzi* with roasted bananas on the side.

Apple Rings in Vanilla Sauce

Apples are a continental favourite brought only recently to Zanzibar, but their crisp, sweet flavour blends easily with vanilla, cardamom and other local spices grown on the island. Although the Zanzibar Serena Inn uses apples in this recipe, the same procedure can be used for other firm fruits like pears and nectarines.

Ingredients
4 apples, peeled, cored and cut into rings
1/2 teaspoon cardamom seeds
1/2 cup sugar
400 ml water
1/4 cup flour
1/2 cup butter for the vanilla sauce
1/2 cup sugar

1 teaspoon vanilla
2 egg yolks
250 ml milk
1/2 teaspoon cardamom seeds

To make the vanilla syrup, cream the sugar and yolks in a small saucepan and mix in the remaining ingredients. Cook, stirring constantly, over moderate heat until slightly thickened. Set aside to cool.

Place the cardamom seeds, sugar and water into a saucepan and bring to the boil. Blanch the apple rings in the cardamom syrup for a few minutes until they begin to soften, then drain and cool. Dredge the apples in flour, then melt the butter in a pan and fry the rings until golden brown. Serve the apple rings covered in the vanilla sauce.

The Palms

The Palms prides itself on personal service and elegant cuisine, mixing international specialities with a contemporary touch. Owned by the Raguz family, sisters Paulina and Nathalie constantly experiment with the best the island has to offer. Eating in such surroundings is always an adventure. Each day at noon, the chef waits on the beach to select the evening meal and the catch of the day from local fishermen returning from that morning's trip on small *ngalawa*, dugout catamarans that travel far into the distant ocean. In the afternoon, gardeners scale tall coconut palms to fetch ripe fruit, breaking open the shaggy husks to reveal sweet, hard flesh and watery milk – the perfect snack after a long day in the sun.

The dining area is enclosed with wall-to-wall windows that overlook the beach front outside. Panels of carved leaves and flowers spread beautiful shadows on tables cloaked in white linen. Meals can be eaten anywhere, from the privacy of your veranda to the shade of beachfront *banda* shelters. The food arrives in coconut shells, hollowed-out passion fruits and local gourds. Banana leaves often form the base of an appetiser or entree and lime blossoms garnish steaming portions served from hand-carved wooden bowls.

At The Palms, the day starts with a hearty breakfast of freshly baked pastries and tropical fruit usually eaten in the dining room, where the morning light seeps in through billowing white curtains to envelop everything in an ethereal glow. Cinnamon French toast comes drenched in a syrupy vanilla sauce and the Raguz's home-made muesli uses coconuts that grow behind the dining room. Just before noon, guests lounging by the pool are treated to frozen fruit skewers of mango, pineapple and papaya accompanied by a refreshing cold towel to counter the warm glow of the tropical sun. Dinner is a formal and romantic affair. Waiters in flowing white *kanzu* robes attend to couples whispering over iced cocktails and tall glasses of wine. Brightly coloured linens adorn tables lit only by candles and the stars outside. The Palms serves simple food with elegance – contemporary creations in romantic and stately surroundings.

Lobster and Avocado Salad
Chilli Garlic Prawns in Coriander and Cashew Pesto
Spicy Red Snapper with Saffron Rice
Chilled Passion Fruit Soup with Grand Mariner

Lobster and Avocado Salad

This refreshing salad is a rich starter, the creamy mellowness of yellow-green avocados blending with the sweet piquancy of sautéed lobster. Make sure your avocados are ripe and firm – the skin should indent slightly when you press your finger into it. Unripe avocados, which are biter and completely inedible, should be left in a brown paper bag in the cupboard to ripen.

Ingredients
500 g lobster meat, roughly chopped
4 large avocados
a head of lettuce, shredded
1/2 cup olive oil
juice of one lemon
a handful of fresh coriander, chopped
salt and pepper to taste

Heat a little of the olive oil over medium heat and sauté the lobster meat until well cooked. Season with salt and pepper. Cover and refrigerate. Peel the avocados and cut them into medium-sized pieces. In a large salad bowl, mix the shredded lettuce with the lobster and avocado

pieces. Add the olive oil, chopped coriander and lemon juice and toss well.

Chilli Garlic Prawns in Coriander and Cashew Pesto

This spicy dip blends coriander, a popular herb on the island of Zanzibar, with the oriental flavours of soy sauce, oyster sauce and toasted cashews. Don't shy away from using the full number of chillies for the marinade – deseeded, they loose most of their bite and add a subdued, gentle heat to the garlic and prawns.

Ingredients
20 medium prawns, cleaned and peeled
8 cloves of garlic, minced
4 red chillies, deseeded and chopped
1 tablespoon salt
1 teaspoon black pepper
lime slices, to garnish for the pesto
2 large handfuls of fresh coriander
2 cups cashews
1/2 cup olive oil
1 tablespoon light soy sauce
1 tablespoon oyster sauce
1 teaspoon each salt and black pepper

In a medium bowl, mix the olive oil, garlic, chillies, salt and black pepper. Add the prawns and stir gently, then cover and refrigerate for at least 3 hours.

To make the pesto, roughly chop the coriander and blend it with the cashews in a food processor until the mixture resembles a paste. (To do this by hand, mince the coriander and cashews, then pound them in a mortar and pestle.) Slowly add the olive oil, soy sauce, oyster sauce, salt and pepper.

Heat a grill pan until it sizzles when you drizzle water over it. Lay the prawns evenly around the surface and brush them generously with the marinade as they cook. After a few minutes, when the translucent flesh begins to turn white and a gentle pink, turn them over and cook until firm but still soft. Serve them on a platter with the pesto for dipping, garnished with slices of lime.

Spicy Red Snapper with Saffron Rice

Red snapper is found throughout the Indian Ocean and its light white flesh makes it an ideal complement for a covering of spices and fresh coriander. Saffron rice is a traditionally Arab dish, its delicate scent lending a Middle Eastern influence to this island feast.

Ingredients

4 red snapper fillets, about 200 g each

4 tablespoons butter

2 large handfuls of fresh coriander, chopped

1 red chilli, chopped

2 teaspoons fresh ginger, grated

4 cups breadcrumbs

for the saffron rice

600 g basmati rice

6 cups water

2 pinches of saffron powder or 2 threads saffron

4 tablespoons butter

Preheat the oven to 220°C. In a food processor, pulse the bread crumbs, coriander, chilli, ginger and butter until the mixture is coarse but not too uniform. Heat a griddle pan to very hot and, after seasoning the fish with salt and pepper, sear the fillets for about 1 minute on either side. Remove from the heat and coat in the spicy bread crumb mixture, then place onto a baking tray and bake for 10 minutes or until the topping is a deep golden brown.

For the rice, set the water to boil in a large pot and when it's at full boil, add the basmati and saffron. Cover and turn the burner to its lowest heat. Simmer for 10-15 minutes. The rice is ready when each grain is fluffy and separate, soft on the outside but a bit chewy to the bite. Stir in the butter before serving.

Chilled Passion Fruit Soup with Grand Mariner

This simple soup blends the tart taste of fresh passion fruit with orange and vanilla in a delicious and refreshingly cool dessert. Passion fruit grows on vines around the island of Zanzibar, its wrinkled skin cut open to reveal crunchy black seeds in a glistening orange and yellow pulp.

Ingredients
15 passion fruit
1 cup icing sugar
1 vanilla pod or 1 teaspoon vanilla
1/2 cup Grand Mariner
vanilla ice cream, icing sugar, and fresh mint to garnish

Slice open the passion fruit and empty the fruit into a medium bowl. Cut the vanilla pod in half and scrape the seeds into the pulp with a sharp knife. Add the icing sugar and the Grand Mariner, mixing thoroughly. Taste to adjust the sweetness, but leave the fruit soup slightly tart. Cover and chill for at least 5 hours, then ladle into soup bowls with a scoop of vanilla ice cream. Dust with icing sugar and garnish with a sprig of fresh mint.

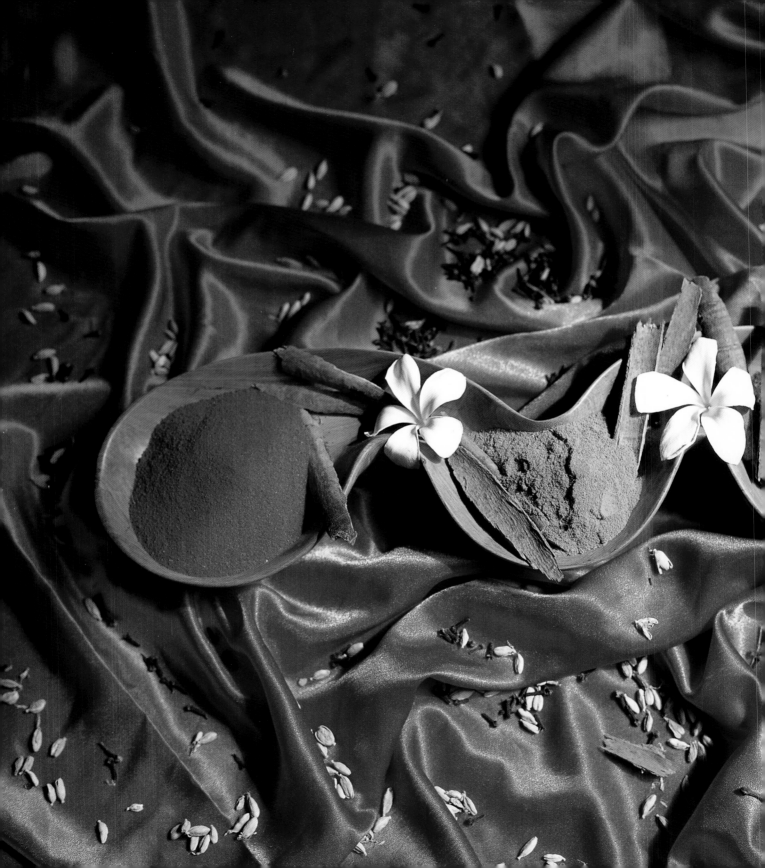

SWAHILI WAY
S p i c e s

Spices play an important role in Swahili cooking. Family recipes for the Indian-influenced *biriyani* – a rice *pilau* with meat and whole pieces of cinnamon bark, clove buds and cardamom seeds cooked slowly over an open fire – are cooked with pride and served during special celebrations. Ginger and lemon grass are steeped in hot water to make a refreshing and astringent tea. Vanilla syrup infused with cardamom coats sweet balls of fried dough called *kaimati* – a popular afternoon snack still sold from food stalls around the Swahili Coast. Since the arrival of Arab traders in Zanzibar, the island has been the seat of spice cultivation throughout the East African coast. Spices were so plentiful on the island that many explorers and travellers, arriving at the port of Stone Town, wrote that before their boat had even landed, the scent of cloves and cinnamon wafted out towards them over the ocean.

Dar es Salaam

Bahari haishi zingo.
An ocean never ceases
to storm.

Ras Kutani

Ras Kutani lies just an hour south of Dar es Salaam, in a quiet bay that feels miles away from the urban city centre that is within commuting distance to its sun-kissed shores. Built in natural style around a quiet lagoon, the property blends the rich environment of the waterway with an untouched Indian Ocean beach to offer an ideal combination of activities and atmosphere. The lodge's style emphasizes natural colours and materials to blend with the richness of the surrounding environment. From the lagoon's peaceful birdlife to the tumultuous waves of the nearby surf, life at Ras Kutani revolves around the water, with views and ocean air playing a large part in the lodge's style.

Most dining takes place in the main area, but Ras Kutani caters for romantic alternatives as well. Meals are served in an open dining room that faces both the beach and the lagoon, where carved seahorses, starfish and shells form creative chair backs and tiles illustrated with marine animals are set into the floor. Down by the beach, a bar made from an old *ngalawa* hull and a thatched *makuti* shelter provide a place where guests can savour a drink in the shade. Couples enjoy private dinners on a small jetty that extends into the lagoon or eat by candlelight on tables set up in the sand.

Meals at the lodge emphasize colour, local produce and pan-African flavours and dishes are a fusion of coastal traditions and popular favourites. Vibrant entrées combine traditional Swahili flavours and continental favourites, like the fish cakes spiced with local mixtures of coriander and cumin seeds below. In keeping with the cooking style of the CC Africa properties of which Ras Kutani is a part, the food is vegetable-based and light, full of healthy goodness and vibrant flavours. The emphasis is on the freshest produce, often grown from the *shamba* gardens of the lodge's staff and picked just that morning. Limes, ginger, garlic, chillies, peppers and coconut all play key parts in the cuisine to emphasize the abundance of the coast, both on land and under the sea.

Seared Tuna with Gazpacho
Swahili Fish Cakes with Sweet Coriander Sauce
Fish Escabeche
Coconut Pancakes with Chocolate Sauce

Seared Tuna with Gazpacho

In hot climates, cold soups and vegetables play an important part in a light and refreshing lunch menu. Here, small pieces of seared tuna – to be cooked as long or as little as you like – bring a coastal flavour to traditional Spanish gazpacho.

Ingredients
2 1/2 cups tomatoes
1 cup cucumber
1/4 cup red onion, minced
1/4 cup yellow pepper
1/4 cup green pepper
1/4 red chilli
1 pinch sugar
1 teaspoon balsamic vinegar
125 ml tomato juice
1 teaspoon olive oil
salt and pepper
200 g tuna fillet

To make the gazpacho, peel the skin from the tomatoes by plunging them into boiling water for a few minutes, draining and carefully removing the skin. Chop them roughly and place in a food processor. Peel, halve and deseed the cucumber, chop it and add it to the tomatoes. Be sure to leave everything chunky. Trim and chop the peppers and chilli, then add it to the food processor mix. Puree until smooth and add the sugar and balsamic vinegar. Transfer the mixture to the serving bowl and whisk in the tomato juice and olive oil. Season and chill for at least an hour before serving.

On a very hot pan, sear the tuna for a few minutes on each side, leaving the interior pink. Slice it into four portions and serve with the soup.

Swahili Fish Cakes with Sweet Coriander Sauce

Fried fish cakes are a popular way of serving white fish. Here, spiced breading adds flavour and an Asian-inspired coriander sauce of ginger, sesame and rice wine vinegar imparts the final touch.

Ingredients

2 eggs
2 tablespoons brown sugar
1/2 red chilli
1 tablespoon paprika
2 cloves of garlic, minced
1 tablespoon lime zest
1/2 tablespoon ground coriander
1/2 ground cumin
1/4 cup fresh coriander, chopped
1 tablespoon fish sauce
1/4 cup lime juice
1/4 cup bread crumbs, plus a little more to coat the fish cakes
vegetable oil, for frying

for the sauce

1/4 cup brown sugar
1/4 cup rice wine vinegar
2 tablespoons ginger, grated
2 tablespoons sesame seeds, toasted
1 teaspoon soy sauce
2 tablespoons fresh coriander, chopped

Puree all the ingredients for the fish cakes in a blender and form small patties by hand. Coat with the rest of the breadcrumbs and fry for 3-4 minutes on each side in vegetable oil over high heat.

To make the sauce, boil the brown sugar, rice vinegar and ginger until thickened. Add the sesame seeds, soy sauce and coriander leaves.

Fish Escabeche

This slightly tart fish salad is a refreshing lunch dish, especially satisfying when served alongside other vegetables dishes and salads. The oregano and vinegar impart a sour hint to the mixture and bright carrots and red onions add colour.

Ingredients

250 g carrots, roughly chopped

2 red onions, sliced

1/4 cup olive oil

2 teaspoons oregano

400 g fish, cut into cubes

1/8 cup white wine vinegar

a pinch of salt

1/4 cup water

5 whole black peppercorns

6 whole coriander seeds

In a large saucepan, fry the onions and carrots in olive oil until soft. Add the coriander, oregano, spices, water and vinegar and boil for 3 minutes. Add the fish and cook for 2 minutes. Season with salt and set aside to cool, stirring the mixture every 15 minutes to keep the flavours evenly distributed.

Coconut Pancakes with Chocolate Sauce

Pancakes with chocolate sauce are a perennial dessert favourite in colder climates. Here, the chefs at Ras Kutani impart a tropical flavour to the combination by adding freshly sliced coconut.

Ingredients

2 cups flour

1 egg

1 tablespoon sugar

3 tablespoons butter, melted

500 ml milk

for the topping

fresh coconut, sliced

1/4 cup chocolate bar, cut into small pieces

1/4 cup orange juice

Mix the flour, egg and sugar until smooth. Slowly add milk until the mixture becomes a smooth batter. Stir in the melted butter. Heat a pan on low heat and pour a quarter of the mixture. Cook until firm on one side, then turn over carefully and cook until golden brown. Remove from heat, fold and cover with topping.

To make the chocolate sauce, melt the chocolate bar and the orange juice in a small saucepan over low heat. Pour it over the cooked pancakes and garnish with slices of fresh coconut.

SWAHILI WAY
The Jiko

Electricity and gas only came to the East African coast within the last century, and even today most Swahili households cook over a charcoal brazier called the *jiko*. A highly versatile cooking stove, the *jiko* is used to cook everything from stacks of light brown *chapati* to simmering *mchuzi* stews. Grilling fish or seafood over a *jiko* is a time-honoured method of preparation and even *dhow* sailors bring a *jiko* along for on-board meals. In villages and towns, *kanga*-clad woman sit near their doorways, turning a whole *samaki* over the charcoal grill. *Jiko* stoves are portable and many entrepreneurs position them at narrow intersections or just outside the local market to sell grilled fish, cassava or maize to passers-by for a mid-afternoon snack. Along the narrow streets of Swahili towns and in the shade of village palm-trees, the aromas from a charcoal *jiko* are always tantalising and full of flavour.

Mafia

Taa haachi mwibawe.
Give a dog a bad name.
"The mud sticks".

Kinasi Lodge

Kinasi Lodge has managed a culinary feat – home cooking on a remote island archipelago, where only rice, cassava, bananas and coconuts grow in abundance under the tropical sun. Dinner is served under Moroccan lanterns overlooking the bay, either in the dining room with its golden ocra walls or on the pool terraces overlooking the beach. Everything from the salt and pepper pots to the wine glasses are an indigo blue, and complete the ocean-and-sun theme adopted in Kinasi's styling.

The bar is an open area of armchairs and reclining benches and generous pillow cushions, where guests can relax as the ocean breeze billows though the sailcloth curtains and rustles the palm trees outside.

Dining at Kinasi is traditional, with guests sitting down to *table d'hote* four-course meals of soup, entree, main course and a fruit-centred dessert. Although fresh vegetables must be shipped or flown in from the mainland, most dishes are flavoured by readily-available ingredients like coconuts, bananas, tomatoes and the catch of the day.

The menus are eclectic and individual, a fusion of Indian Ocean recipes and North African and Mediterranean flavours such as oven-baked lasagne of lobster, coriander and asparagus, lunchtime pizzas topped with fresh seafood, and risottos of local spinach and fresh crab. Swahili food buffets and seafood barbecues are weekly rituals.

Banana trees are abundant on the Swahili Coast, and local *shambas*, or small farms, wouldn't be complete without a few banana trees planted between rows of tomatoes and the local spinach, *mchicha*. And bananas are the culprit in one of Kinasi's great treats, the famous trifle, developed to local ingredients by Jenny Saar, formerly the Chef at Gibb's Farm. She came up with this soothing tropical-island treat and comfort food. It's become a lodge favourite, served in thick earthenware bowls with a generous splash of rum.

Crab and Coconut Soup with Watercress and Coriander
Fried Calamari with Sesame Seeds and Kinasi Tartare Sauce
Grilled Tuna Steaks with fresh Horseradish Salsa
Island Life Banana Trifle

Crab and Coconut Soup with Watercress

Coconut cream compliments the natural sweetness of fresh crab in this smooth and satisfying soup. The green colour of the watercress makes the soup a delicate pale green. Coconut milk can be substituted, but the soup will be thinner and loose it's velvety texture.

Ingredients
3 big crabs
4 tablespoons butter
1/4 cup flour
1 onion, chopped
1 litre coconut cream
1 cube of chicken stock
A small bunch of fresh watercress, chopped
Coriander to flavour and garnish

Plunge the crabs into a large pot of salted boiling water and cook for about 10 minutes. Let them cool, then crack open with a large hammer or rolling pin and remove the meat from the centre and claws.

In a large saucepan, heat the butter and add the onion, stirring constantly for about five minutes, or until the onion is translucent and beginning to turn a lovely golden colour. Add the coconut cream, flour and stock cube, bringing the mixture to the boil on low heat. Let the mixture simmer, without covering it, for about 20 minutes, stirring occasionally to keep the coconut cream from sticking to the bottom of the pan.

Add the crabmeat little by little, then throw in the watercress and simmer for another 5 minutes. When the watercress is wilted and beginning to disintegrate, it's ready to serve.

Fried Calamari with Sesame Seeds and Kinasi Tartare Sauce

Fried calamari is a Mediterranean favourite, and the use of coconut cream in the tartar sauce lends the dish a coastal flavour. Go to the extra effort to make Kinasi's special tartare sauce, which uses coconut cream instead of eggs - it's worth it.

Ingredients

500 g calamari, cleaned and cut into one-centimetre strips
2 eggs
1 cup bread crumbs
1/3 cup sesame seeds
vegetable oil, for frying
1/4 cup olive oil
the juice of 3 limes
1 tablespoon fresh coriander, chopped
1/2 teaspoon salt
a pinch of sugar

for Kinasi's special tartar sauce:

1/4 cup coconut cream
1/4 cup yoghurt
1 cup mayonnaise
1 tomato, deseeded and chopped finely
1/2 onion, chopped finely
1/2 green pepper, chopped finely
1/4 cucumber, chopped finely
2 garlic cloves, crushed
1 tablespoon fresh ginger, grated
2 tablespoons Worchester sauce
1/2 teaspoon paprika

Combine the olive oil, lime, coriander, salt and sugar in a large bowl. Mix in the calamari strips, marinating them for half and hour. Beat the eggs into the calamari marinade and in a separate bowl, mix the breadcrumbs and sesame seeds together. In a wok or a large frying pan, heat a generous amount of vegetable oil (at least two fingers' height) to the point where when you drip some water in, the oil sizzles and spits. Take a few pieces of the marinated calamari and dip them in the breadcrumb mixture, being sure to coat the pieces on both sides. Slide them into the hot oil with a slotted spoon and fry in small batches - if you put to many in, the oil's temperature will decrease and they won't be crispy - until golden brown, and remove them carefully to drain on kitchen paper. As you're frying, mix the ingredients for the tartar sauce in a bowl and serve with the calamari strips, piping hot and piled onto a large plate.

Grilled Tuna with Horseradish

Try to get Yellowfin tuna or Dog-tooth tuna fillets for this. Wahoo and Trevalley are also superb fish for this method.

Whether you choose to marinate the tuna before grilling it is largely up to you, but the mustard and lime marinade goes so well with soft pink of the steaks that it's worth it, but do not marinate for more than five minutes. The sauce requires refrigerating in advance, but don't skip it – you'll want lots.

Ingredients
4 250 g tuna steaks
1/2 cup soy sauce
1/4 cup Dijon mustard
1/3 cup lime juice
2 garlic cloves, crushed
1 teaspoon lemon zest
2 tablespoons honey
for the sauce:
1 cup whipped cream
1/3 cup freshly grated horseradish
1 teaspoon sugar
1/4 cup fresh green pepper, minced finely

To make the sauce, combine all the ingredients in a large bowl and refrigerate for an hour before serving. In another bowl, mix the soy sauce, mustard, lime juice, garlic, lemon zest and honey and add the tuna steaks, making sure they're covered with the marinade. Let them rest for about half an hour, but if you're stretched for time, five minutes will do. Preheat a grill until it sizzles violently when you sprinkle water over it. Grill the tuna steaks, two at a time if there's not enough space for all of them at once, for 5 to 7 minutes on each side, then turn and grill the same amount of time. The grill will leave lovely black lines on the steaks, which will be charred on the outside and – provided you don't overcook it – still just pink on the inside. Serve with the sauce.

Banana Bread Trifle

This recipe should be made well in advance and chilled before serving, and you don't have to use banana bread – the usual sponge fingers will do. But if you want the sweet, comforting taste of bananas times infinity, it has to be made with banana bread. Really ripe bananas are best here.

Ingredients

Banana bread:

225 g flour

1$^{1/2}$ teaspoons baking powder

1/2 teaspoon salt

110 g butter, softened

225 g sugar

110 g raisins

30 g nuts, chopped

2 eggs

4 cups mashed bananas

for the trifle:

1 loaf banana bread, cut into one-centimetre slices

500 ml milk

3 tablespoons custard powder

1/4 cup sugar

2 egg yolks

1 tot sherry, plus a little for sprinkling

2 tots rum, plus a little for sprinkling

4 large bananas, cut into thin rounds

To make the banana bread, preheat the oven to 160°C. Cream the butter and sugar together, then add the flour, baking powder and salt. With a wooden spoon, stir until everything is mixed and not lumpy, but don't over beat. Add the nuts, eggs and mashed bananas, and mix well. Pour into a buttered loaf tin and bake for 45 minutes to an hour, until the bread is brown on top and fall easily out of its tin.

To make the custard for the trifle, heat the milk in a saucepan until almost boiling and add the custard powder, sugar and egg yolks. Stir until well blended and add the sherry and rum. Spoon a layer of custard into a glass bowl and top it with a layer of the banana bread fingers. Sprinkle a bit of sherry and rum on top of the bread to moisten it, then top with a layer of fresh bananas. Repeat this once or twice until the custard and the banana bread has run out, the sprinkle again with rum and sherry, and finish it off with more fresh banana rounds. Refrigerate the trifle for an hour or more to let the flavours fuse, then serve directly from the glass bowl, dishing servings out at the table.

Chole Mjini

Located in such castaway seclusion, meals at Chole Mjini involve adaptation and improvisation on a daily basis. The menus are a careful result of endless experimentation by owners Jean and Anne de Villiers, who have scoured the island to incorporate local ingredients and traditional cooking into the lodge's repertoire of culinary feats. When the property first opened, all the cooking was done over open fires on a tiled brick barbecue that has now become a main feature of the common area. These days, the kitchen is just behind the path to the dining room and the faint smell of scented smoke from wood fires in the late morning and early evening announces that the food is well on its way.

Chole lies just off the larger land mass of Mafia and groves of fruit trees left from the days of Swahili merchants and their plantations still produce a seasonal crop of lemons and oranges, mangoes and avocados all over the small island. Behind the shoreline and the tree houses, raised platforms of vegetables and herbs grow in the shade of towering palms. Each morning, village fishermen bring their catch to the kitchen doors for Daima, the head cook, to choose from, picking wide-eyed fish and ivory-coloured calamari from their woven *kikapu* baskets. The selected ones will end up curried, fried or even baked in a pesto of *mboga ya pwani*, a seaside pursulane that grows close to the ocean shore. At low tide, women bring buckets of writhing octopus to tenderise on the rocky shore, beating the purplish tentacles to a smooth, soft white.

Dinner at Chole Mjini is the quintessential experience. Where else can you enjoy a three-course meal between the tumbling walls of an old merchant's house, geckos scampering over the blackened coral as you step through the abandoned doorway? A short barefoot walk through the sand leads to an enchanted enclosure of romantic indulgence. Twinkling lanterns hang from the twisted roots of old strangler figs slowly consuming the abandoned house, and as one course follows another, it's hard not to image the flavours and rhythms of life on this island centuries ago.

Green Bean and Cashew Salad
Lemon Papaya Soup
Octopus Mchuzi with Chapatti
Lemon Coconut Tart with Ginger Tea

Green Bean and Cashew Salad

Cashew trees grown all over Chole island – reminders of the Arab presence that dominated the area only a century ago. Be sure not to overcook the beans – it ruins the texture of this crunchy salad.

Ingredients
600 g tender green beans, topped and tailed
1 red onion, sliced thinly
1 cup toasted cashews
1/2 cup vinaigrette dressing

Before you blanch the beans, be sure to have a large bowl of ice-cold water ready. Bring a large pot of salted water to the boil and when it's bubbling fiercely, plunge in the green beans. Let them cook for 3-5 minutes, until just tender but still crisp. Drain them and immediately plunge into the ice water. Drain again and add them to the serving bowl with the onions, cashews and vinaigrette dressing. Toss until well mixed and serve.

Lemon Papaya Soup

This cold soup uses papaya, a common fruit on the Swahili Coast, as a savoury ingredient. Usually served for breakfast with a slice of lime, in this recipe the flavour of the papaya is brought out with citrus juices and deepened with the addition of cumin, ginger and chilli.

Ingredients
1 large ripe papaya
1 cup citron, lemon or lime juice
1 cup orange juice
3 cloves of garlic, chopped
1 teaspoon cumin powder
1 teaspoon powdered ginger
1/2 teaspoon chilli powder
1 teaspoon black pepper
1 teaspoon salt
chopped fresh coriander and croutons, to garnish

Mix all of the ingredients together in a blender until smooth. Chill and serve topped with chopped fresh coriander and croutons.

Octopus Mchuzi with Chapatti

Octopus, or *pweza* in Swahili, is a favourite ingredient on Chole Island. At low tide, agile women spear octopuses by hand and quickly kill them before they attach their tentacles to their outstretched arms and try to bite. Since the Indian community brought their cooking styles and flavours to the East African coast long ago, *chapatis* have become a mainstay of the Swahili diet. Roadside stalls sell fresh *chapatis* to workers during morning tea breaks, and most meals come with a folded *chapati* on the side of the plate, steaming hot from the pan.

Ingredients
1 kg octopus
4 tablespoons vegetable oil

500 ml coconut milk
one 225 g tin of tomato paste water
1 teaspoon salt
1 teaspoon turmeric
2 onions, minced
1 green pepper, minced
4 tomatoes, minced
6 cloves of garlic, minced
1 stalk lemon grass
1 tablespoon ginger, grated
juice of 1 lime and its zest
for the chapati
2 tablespoons vegetable oil, plus more for the pan
water
1 teaspoon salt
500 g wheat flour
1 tablespoon butter or margarine

In a large pot, boil the octopus for about 30 minutes or until soft. Drain, cool and cut into bite-sized pieces. Set aside. Heat the oil in a large saucepan and sauté the onions, green peppers and tomatoes until they begin to soften. Add half the coconut milk and the turmeric powder and cook until the vegetables are tender. Add the garlic, ginger, lime zest and the stalk of lemon grass, tied into a bundle to prevent it from dispersing its tough leaves throughout the stew. Simmer for 5-10 minutes, then add the rest of the coconut milk, the lime juice and salt to taste. Add the octopus, stir until it's well heated and serve with the *chapati*.

To make the *chapati*, mix the flour, salt, butter and vegetable oil in a large bowl. Add a tablespoon of water at a time as you knead the dough. Once it holds together in a large - but not too sticky - ball, divide the dough into four parts and smear them with a little oil to keep them from getting dry. On a floured board, roll each ball into rounds about 1/4 cm thick. Heat an oiled frying pan over medium heat and when hot, slide a *chapati* into the pan. After 1 minute, turn it over and cook for the same amount of time – the *chapati* should be golden with spots of brown on the both sides. If it starts to stick, add a little more oil to the pan, but not too much – the *chapatis* should cook slowly, not fry. Keep them covered and warm until serving time.

Lemon Coconut Tart with Ginger Tea.
Lemon trees grow all over Mafia and Chole Island, and form the basis of many of Chole Mjini's desserts and cakes. This lemon tart was so popular with the cooking staff that they make it back in the village for their husbands and children on special holidays. Ginger, or *tangawizi* in Swahili, is the only ingredient in this gentle tea used to calm the stomach and aid digestion.

Ingredients
for the crust
1 1/2 cup butter
2 tablespoons sugar

one egg yolk

for the filling

2 or 3 tablespoons water

1/2 cup lemon juice

2 tablespoons lemon zest

5 eggs, separated

1 cup sugar

200 ml cream

1/2 cup milk

2 cups grated coconut

for the ginger tea

1 litre water

4 tablespoons fresh ginger, grated

sugar to taste

Preheat the oven to 180°C. Mix the butter, sugar and egg yolk together to form a soft dough and try handle it as little as possible. If the dough is too sticky, add a bit more flour but if it's too dry, add some butter or milk.

Cover the dough and let it rest in the refrigerator for 20 minutes. Lay greaseproof or wax paper on a counter and, adding flour to keep the dough from sticking, roll out the pastry until it's thin enough to line the bottom and sides of a 22-cm pie tin. Carefully, flip the greaseproof paper upside-down into the tart shell and push the edges of the pastry into the corners of the tin. Carefully peel off the paper and bake the shell blind for about 12 minutes, or until it's just starting to colour.

Mix all of the ingredients for the filling in a large bowl and, leaving the tart shell in the oven, carefully pour it in – this way it's less likely to spill as you carry it to the oven. Bake at 180°C for about 40-45 minutes, or until the filling is set but still a bit soft.

To make the tea, bring the water to the boil in a large saucepan and add the grated ginger. Let it simmer for a few minutes and taste it, adding sugar to taste. Strain and serve hot.

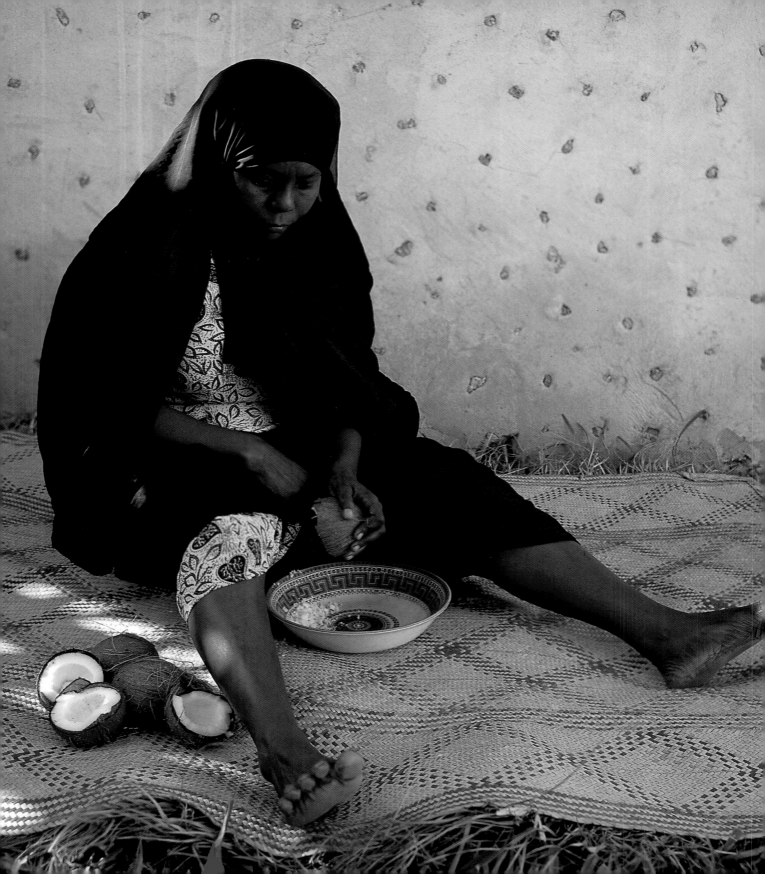

SWAHILI WAY
Coconut Milk

The coconut, or *nazi* in Swahili, is a staple of life along the East African coast. The coconut palm grows abundantly throughout the tropics and is used extensively as a source of food and a natural material for everything from house roofs to fishing traps. Unripe coconuts called *madafu* are harvested while they are still green, well before a matted brown husk forms around the outer shell. The *madafu* are cut open with a sharp machete and sold to drink, while the mature *nazi* coconuts are grated and used for cooking everything from coconut rice to mchuzi stew. Harvesting coconuts from the tall palms is a daunting experience – adult trees can grow up to 50 metres high. Using a woven *mkeka* strap, brave young men levy their way up to the top of the palms and with a large stick knock the fruit down to the waiting ground below.

Glossary

bhajia – fried balls of cooked lentils and vegetables, flavoured with coriander and other spices; a favourite snack food

biriyani – a festival dish of meat or fish-flavoured sauce served with spiced rice

chai – black tea, often served with plenty of milk and sugar

changu – a type of fish found around the Swahili coast

chapati – flat bread of Indian origin made from whole-wheat flour and cooked over a flame

dagaa – small either dried or fresh fish usually cooked in a stew.

embe – mango

halua – a traditional Arab sweet of flavoured sugar with a consistency like Turkish delight; can also be made of mashed dates flavoured with spices

jiko – a small charcoal brazier stove

jikoni – the kitchen

kiwe la kupazia – a round stone on which grains are ground by hand

jiwe la kusaga dawa – an oblong stone on which medicinal herbs are ground by hand

kamba – prawns

kaimati – sweet balls of fried dough spiced with cardamom and served in a sweet syrup

kunguto – woven cylindrical container used for squeezing and straining coconut milk

kikapu – a basket woven from sisal or palm fronds used for carrying all sorts of things

kinu – a small mortar, usually carved from wood

kioski – a small shop selling food and other implements

kinu cha tambi – a wooden press used for squeezing vermicelli-like noodles

konde – plantations outside of town where food for the household is grown

kupika – to cook

mahamri – sweet spiced doughnuts

maharagwe – kidney-shaped beans, a staple of the Swahili diet

majani ya pwani – an edible green that grows on the beach

maandazi – spiced triangle-shaped dough flavoured with cardamom and fried

marekani – thin cotton cloth, usually sold by the roll

masala – a blend of mixed spices

masala chai – sweet, milky black tea spiced with a mixture of ginger, cinnamon and black pepper

mbaazi – lentils cooked in coconut cream and tomatoes, a Swahili breakfast favourite

mboga – vegetables

mbuzi – a small wooden stool with a serrated blade on one end used for grating coconut

mchele – uncooked white rice

mchicha – local greens cooked like spinach

mchuzi – a spiced stew or curry made from a base of meat, seafood, or vegetables

mezze – a style of serving appetisers that originated in the Middle East, many small bowls of different dishes arrive to be eaten simultaneously with fresh bread

mkate wa mafuta – a loaf bread made from white flour cooked in oil

mishkaki – skewers of meat, chicken or fish, sometimes spiced, grilled over charcoal

mkaa – charcoal

mkeka – thin mats woven by hand from thin palm fronds

mkwaju – tamarind

mofa – flat sourdough bread made from millet and corn

mtungi – a clay pot used to store water

mzee – an elderly man and a term of respect in Swahili culture

ndizi – banana

nyama – meat, usually beef

pilau – rice cooked with whole spices

pojo – green lentils cooked in a mixture of spices

pweza – octopus

samaki – fish

samaki wa kupaka – whole fish grilled in cumin, pepper, cinnamon, tamarind and coconut cream

samosa – fried triangular pockets of spiced beef or vegetables; a favourite snack food

shamba – a farm or orchard of varying sizes where people farm for subsistence and sell the excess in their local market

siki – vinegar distilled from assorted ingredients

sufuria – a metal cooking pot

taarab – a traditional oriental music composed by the Swahili community. Taraab music has been profoundly influenced by the drumming styles of Egypt and the Arab world, where many of its founding musicians studied

tamarind – found throughout the Middle East, East Africa and the Indian Ocean, the tamarind tree's fruit grows within a sticky pod

tangawizi – ginger

Tinga-tinga – a colourful style of painting animals and village scenes pioneered in Dar es Salaam by Edward Saidi Tinga-tinga and now popular throughout the East African coast

uji – a thin maize meal porridge commonly eaten for breakfast

uteo – a wooden object used in making baskets

wali – cooked white rice

Acknowledgments

A cookbook about any culture's cuisine is invariably a collection - a shared endeavour of cook and eater alike. Many hours in the kitchen, many smiling mouths and full bellies went into the making of this book, and while we can't thank everyone by name, we would like to try.

In Lamu a special thanks to Pierre and Mwanashee Oberson at Kijani and Lars and Carol Korschen at Peponi. At Kiwayu, Mike Kennedy, Cinda Rumbold for recording each and every detail and Chef William Kahindi and Tima Kombo in the kitchen. Leslie Duckworth and Angelika Schuetz at Shela, Palm and Beach House, Mark and Richenda Eddy on Tusitiri Dhow, Eric and Chef Raymond Karima at Kipungani, and Gillies Turles and Fiammetta Monicelli at Fatuma's Tower.

In Mombasa, Fabrizio and Marika Molinaro and Chef Thomas Kilonzo of Alfajiri. At the Serena, Mugo Maringa for his invaluable assistance and Chef Harun Njoka for his unwavering professionalism and commitment to the craft. Thanks also to Alessandro and Claudia Torriani at Funzi Keys and Hugh Walters, Jerome and Charlotte at The Tamarind Dhow. A special thanks to Ute and Crispin Sassoon for putting everything together at the eleventh hour.

On the Tanzanian coast, a special thanks to Peter and Antonella Byrnes of Kinasi and Anne and Jean de Villiers of Chole Mjini. Also to Mwalimu Ally at Ras Kutani .

In Zanzibar, thanks to Stephanie and Nathalie Raguz and Adriano at The Palms, Chef Roy at the Serena. A special thanks to Shinuna Karume for her time and hospitality.

Finally, a thanks to all the family and friends who patiently signed each time we travelled again, a special thanks to Kulsum Jafferji for her styling and food assistance and many thanks to Maarten Boeye for being a patient taster and keeping me company in the kitchen.

Contact Addresses

LAMU

Beach House
P.O. Box 39486
Nairobi 00623, Kenya
Tel (254) 20 4442171
Fax (254) 20 4445010
shela@africaonline.co.ke
www.lamu-shela.com or
www.shelahouse.com

Fatuma's Tower
P.O. Box 323
Lamu, Kenya
Bookings through Monika
Fauth
Tel (254) 42-632-044
banana@africaonline.co.ke
Proprietor Gillies Turle
Tel (254) 42 632079
gillies@africaonline.co.ke
www.yogalamu.com

Kijani House Hotel
P.O. Box 266
Lamu, Kenya
Tel (254) 42 633235/6/7 or
733 616231
Fax (254) 42 633374
kijani@africaonline.co.ke
www.kijani-house.com

Kipungani Explorer
Heritage Management Limited
P.O. Box 74888
Nairobi 00200, Kenya
Tel (254) 20 4446651 or
4447929
Fax (254) 20 4446600 or
4446533
sales@heritagehotels.co.ke
www.heritage-eastafrica.com

Munira's Island Camp
P.O. Box 40088 G.P.O.
Nairobi 00100, Kenya
Tel (254) 20 512213 or
733 583-627/963-813
Fax (254) 20-512-543
bigblue@africaonline.co.ke
www.kiwayuisland.com

Peponi Hotel
P.O. Box 24
Lamu 80500, Kenya
Tel (254) 42 633421/3/4 or
633154
Mobile (254) 722 203082 or
734 203082
Fax (254) 42-633-029
peponi@africaonline.co.ke
www.peponi-lamu.com

Tusitiri Dhow
P.O. Box 24498
Nairobi 00502, Kenya
Tel (254) 733 649833
tusitiridhow@africaonline.co.ke

MOMBASA

Alfajiri Villas
P.O. Box 454
Ukinda, Kenya
Tel (254) 40 3202630
Fax (254) 40 3202218
molinaro@africaonline.co.ke
www.alfajirivillas.com

The Funzi Keys
International Reservations
Orion Park
Northfield Avenue
London W13 9SJ
United Kingdom
Tel 020 8840 2900
Fax 020 8840 2950
funzikeys@aboutafrica.co.uk
www.thefunzikeys.com

**Mombasa Serena Beach
Hotel**
P.O. Box 90352
Mombasa, Kenya
Tel (254) 41 5485721/2/3
Fax (254) 41 5485453
mombasa@serena.co.ke
www.serenahotels.com

The Moorings
Mtwapa Creek
P.O. Box 10294
Bamburi
Mombasa, Kenya
Tel (254) 722 411812 or
733 425402
sassooncrispin@email.com

The Tamarind Dhow
P.O. Box 85785
Mombasa, Kenya
Tel (254) 41 474600/1/2/10
Fax (254) 41 474630 or 471948
dhow@tamarindmsa.co.ke
www.tamarind.co.ke

ZANZIBAR

The Palms
P.O. Box 1361
Zanzibar, Tanzania
Tel (255) 747 415049
Fax (255) 741 333151
thepalms@africaonline.co.tz
info@palms-zanzibar.com
www.palms-zanzibar.com

Zanzibar Serena Inn
P.O. Box 4151
Zanzibar, Tanzania
Tel (255) 24 2233587
Fax (255) 24 2233019
zserena@zanzinet.com
www.serenahotels.com

DAR ES SALAAM

Ras Kutani
Box 1192 Dar es Salaam,
Tanzania
Tel: (255) 22 2134794
Fax: (255) 22 2112794
info@selous.com
www.selous.com

MAFIA

Chole Mjini
2chole@bushmail.net
cholemjini@africatravelresource.com

Kinasi Lodge
P.O. Box 18033
Dar es Salaam, Tanzania
Tel (255) 741 324463 or
744 481033
Fax (255) 24 2238220
kinasi@zanlink.com
www.mafiaisland.com

*The following airlines provide
internal flights within Tanzania and
Kenya.*

Air Kenya
P.O. Box 30357
Nairobi, Kenya
Tel (254) 20 601727 or 601734
Fax (254) 20 602951
resvns@airkenya.com
www.airkenya.com

Coastal Travels Ltd.
P.O. Box 3052
Dar es Salaam, Tanzania
Tel (255) 22 2117959/60
Fax (255) 22 2118647
aviation@coastal.cc
www.coastal.cc

The Photographer

Javed Jafferji studied photography, film and television in the UK, before returning to Tanzania to publish various books, including Historical Zanzibar - Romance of the Ages; Images of Zanzibar; Zanzibar Stone Town - an Architectural Exploration; Zanzibar - an Essential Guide; Tanzania - African Eden, A Taste of Zanzibar, Zanzibar Style, Zanzibar Style Recipes, Safari Living, Safari Living Recipes and Swahili Style.

His work has been published in national and international newspapers and magazines including The Times, Newsweek and Geo. He has held exhibitions in London, Paris, Berlin and Pakistan as well as Tanzania.

Javed also publishes a magazine called 'The Swahili Coast' to promote eco-tourism in Tanzania, manages a photography and design studio and runs a gift shop, the Zanzibar Gallery, which sells gifts, clothes, books and antiques.

The Writer

Elie Losleben graduated from the American University in Cairo with a BA. She has written two educational books for children, *The Bedouin of the Middle East* and *Libya* as well as contributed to several international publications in the U.K., East Africa and the Middle East including *Harpers & Queen* and *Travel Today*. Losleben was raised in Cairo and enjoys travelling in Africa and the Arab world. "It was fascinating to observe the similarities between Swahili and Arab culture," she says. "In the old towns of Lamu and Zanzibar, you can feel a palpable connection to the Arab world." She lives in New York City.